A STUDY OF
CHINESE COMMUNES
1965

By
Shahid Javed Burki

中國人民公社調查

Harvard East Asian Monographs

HARVARD EAST ASIAN MONOGRAPHS
29

A STUDY OF CHINESE COMMUNES
1965

A STUDY OF CHINESE COMMUNES, 1965

by

Shahid Javed Burki

Published by
East Asian Research Center
Harvard University

Distributed by
Harvard University Press
Cambridge, Mass.
1969

Copyright, 1969, by
the President and Fellows of
Harvard College

The East Asian Research Center at Harvard
University administers research projects designed
to further scholarly understanding of China, Korea,
Japan, and adjacent areas. These studies have been
assisted by grants from the Ford Foundation.

Library of Congress No. 73-82301
SBN   674-85310-5

TO *Abaii*

Foreword

Although communes have been the basic units of economic and political organization in rural China since 1958, outsiders have found it extremely difficult to obtain a first-hand impression of them. In 1958 and 1959 the Chinese government released ample statistics, but later it acknowledged that the figures had been exaggerated. Since that time the Chinese government has published virtually no data on commune production, and not many foreigners have been allowed to see communes, except for a few model institutions in urban areas.

In the summer of 1965 a three-man delegation from the government of Pakistan was given a rare opportunity to study Chinese communes. Mr. Shahid Javed Burki, then Director of West Pakistan's Rural Work Programme, was a member of this delegation. Mr. Burki spent nearly six weeks in China, visiting communes, holding discussions with their officials, and collecting data on their agricultural production. There is every reason to believe that the data he received were the same as those the commune officials were themselves using in their record books as a basis for their planning.

Mr. Burki was a Rhodes Scholar at Oxford University from 1961 to 1963. He was appointed Director of the Rural Works Programme in West Pakistan in 1964. This monograph was written in 1967 and 1968 while he was a student at Harvard in a seminar taught by Professor Dwight Perkins at the Kennedy School of Government.

Ezra F. Vogel
East Asian Research Center

PREFACE

In June 1965, I was a member of a three-man delegation from Pakistan which went to Peking to study Chinese communes. We stayed in China for nearly six weeks, visited thirteen communes located in one autonomous region, two municipalities, and five provinces. In Peking, we met with officials from the Chinese Ministries and Bureaus of Agriculture, Animal Husbandry, Commune Management, Finance, and Economic Planning. In Huhehot, Shenyang, Changchun, Hangchow, Wusih, Shanghai, and Canton, we held meetings with officials from the provincial departments of economic development and agricultural planning. In Huhehot, Peking, and Shanghai the delegation requested and had special visits arranged to the Inner Mongolian Animal Husbandry and Agriculture College, the Peking Academy of Agricultural Sciences and the Shanghai Agriculture University. In Shenyang we visited a factory producing pumping equipment for use in the agriculture sector; in Changchun we saw a huge lorry factory producing vehicles which were used by the communes for hauling agricultural produce to the markets and bringing back inputs like chemical fertilizers and insecticides from the cities; in Shanghai we spent one full day in a tractor-and-agricultural machinery complex which supplies most of the Central and South Chinese communes, and in Canton we paid a visit to a newly commissioned chemical fertilizer factory producing 150,000 tons of ammonium sulphate and allied products.

When we reached Peking, we had very little idea of what to see in China. None of us knew Chinese. In fact all we knew about China herself had been hastily picked up from the few books available in the library of the Pakistan Ministry of Information, in Rawalpindi. After we came together in May, barely a month before our departure for China, we had very little time to work together. We only knew that a job had to be done and a report had to be

ix

submitted to the government of Pakistan, explaining the working of the communes in China. Very little preliminary work was done before reaching China; the only significant decison taken about the report was that it would be divided into three parts. Mr. Ihsanul Haq, the leader of the delegation, was entrusted with the task of analyzing the political and sociological aspects of the communes, and Mr. Khorshed Alam with the administrative structure of the communes and the role of the government cadres in commune management. I was assigned the task of analyzing the economic factors which led to the formation of communes in China and also determining the impact of communization on the Chinese economy.

When the delegation re-formed in Peking (our leader's arrival in Peking was delayed by one week), we knew the job that had to be done but had very little idea of the way we should go about it. We, therefore, left most of the planning of our time in China to officials of the Bureau of Commune Management. The bureau took two days to chalk out a very elaborate program which included visits to about twenty communes in the five provinces of Kirin, Liaoning, Kiangsu, Chekiang and Kwangtung and in the two municipalities of Peking and Shanghai. In the discussions that followed, the bureau officials agreed to make four important changes in the program. First, they offered to show us a commune in an underdeveloped region of the country (we suggested a visit to Sinkiang but they decided to take us to Inner Mongolia instead). Second, they accepted our proposal of visits to some of the academic institutions engaged in agricultural work. Third, they agreed to show us some industries considered crucial for agricultural development. Finally, they agreed to leave the choice of communes to provincial level officials. We were asked to pick at random the names of two communes from a list to be prepared by the bureaus of commune management in all the provinces we were scheduled to visit.

During our forty-day stay in China, we spent a total of 313 hours in ninety-seven different meetings. Of these, thirteen meetings were held with the members of various commune management committees, eight with the members of production brigade management committees, and eleven with the leaders of production teams. The delegation spent 18 hours in eight meetings talking to various officials connected with commune affairs and held twenty-four meetings discussing various aspects of communization. We also held eleven sessions in various academic institutions and went to nine meetings arranged by the officials working in industries supporting agricultural development. By the time the delegation was ready to leave China, we had collected an enormous amount of data on various aspects of communization. Most of the data were given voluntarily by the Chinese officials and some were obtained when we made specific requests to the concerned ministries, departments, and bureaus.

The present study was undertaken by the author at the suggestion of Professors Dwight E. Perkins and Subramanian Swamy of the Department of Economics of Harvard University and this book would not have been written without their encouragement and advice. It is, in fact, an expanded version of a paper read in a seminar organized by them in the spring of 1968. Both men devoted many hours of their valuable time to help me solve difficulties occasioned by the sorting of data in an extremely raw form. I have also benefited tremendously from the comments of Professor Ezra Vogel and Professor John Pelzel on an earlier draft of the paper.

This study relies heavily on my personal file; for the sake of preserving consistency, no data, even when they were available, have been taken from other sources. I have deliberately avoided making references to or quoting from other works on the same subject.

An appendix contains some useful information on the communes that I visited. To make cross-reference easier, this material has been presented under seventeen sub-heads. In referring to this data in the main body of the text I have used the number of the commune and the number of the subheading. Thus (VII, 8) means the entry under "Bureaucracy" for Hsin Lung San Commune. The Appendix is a faithful transcription of the interviews held with officials of the thirteen communes visited by the delegation. All the information contained therein has been presented in the present tense and refers to the summer of 1965.

CONTENTS

TABLES

Chapter I

ORGANIZATION AND REORGANIZATION

Formation of the Communes

The first step toward the communization of Chinese agriculture was taken by some cadres working in Sui-p'ing county of Honan province. These cadres formed a federation of 27 Advanced Agricultural Producers' Cooperatives, and the management of the pooled resources of the old cooperatives was taken over by a committee chosen democratically by the people. Thus was born the first Chinese commune in April, 1958. This step toward communization received the Chinese Communist Party's official blessing in August, 1958. The rush that followed resulted in the conversion of over 700,000 Advanced Agricultural Producers' Cooperatives into 24,000 People's Communes. The first phase of communization was over before the end of 1958; the next phase was to take more than three years to complete.

The setting up of communes in China's agricultural sector was a major surgical operation, carried out under the blinding light of national publicity and at a breathtaking speed. In four months, the entire face of Chinese agriculture had been transformed beyond recognition. The national newspapers paid glowing tributes to the cadres and peasants who had worked fast to set up communes in their areas and this public recognition added more speed to the whole operation. Why did the Chinese show such haste in reorganizing their agricultural sector, particularly when the initial steps had been taken at a relatively leisurely pace? To this question, the Chinese officials have a very simple answer.

According to them, a long leap is always better than a short step. The forward leap makes it possible to test the full potential of the move; it is always possible to consolidate the new position by moving backward, inch by inch, here and there. The agricultural sector was successfully communized in the period 1958-1961; the leap forward came in the last quarter of 1958 and the inching backward was accomplished in the years 1959, 1960, and 1961. However, the phase of consolidation would not have taken so long but for three factors.

Reorganization of the Communes

First, this period coincided with that of country-wide drought and bad harvests. Some official energy that would have been devoted to streamlining the commune system was spent instead on making food available to the critical areas. Second, immediately after the completion of the first phase of communization, enormous expenditures were made for land reclamation and water conservancy projects. Reorganization involved the dismantling of many old communes and the creation of thousands of new ones. The division of assets and liabilities between the new communes was a complicated process involving a great deal of official time. We saw an example of this in Northeast China. (See Appendix: VI,7). Third, the earlier communes were formed by the local cadres. Later communes were demarcated by officials belonging to county and provincial administrations. In 1958, the cadres had formed communes out of cooperatives simply by producing consensus among the leaders of the federating units. The new communes of the 1959-1961 period were formed out of old communes on the basis of geographical, economical, and social contiguity. The latter process necessarily took a longer time.

The period between 1959 and 1961 was admittedly a bad one for Chinese agriculture. The officials from the Ministry of Agriculture and Bureau of Commune Management are, however, firmly convinced that the plummeting of agricultural production in this period had absolutely nothing to do with communization. In fact, according to them, the country would have faced a far graver crisis than it actually did, had the communes not been formed in the year 1958. The fact that the country pulled itself up so quickly after 1961 was cited as a proof of the effectiveness of the system of communes.

Considerations in the Formation of the Communes

Why was the process of communization begun in 1958? The First Five
Year Plan, which was completed in 1957, had laid greater stress on industrialization than on the development of agriculture. In the Second Five Year
Plan, launched in 1958, the Communist Party laid down the policy of "socialist
construction" in a much bigger way. A greater balance was needed in the
growth of the economy and as such an upsurge was required in agricultural
production. This in turn meant a massive investment in land improvement
and water conservancy projects. Much of this work had to be done by human
labor without any assistance from machines. An Advanced Agricultural Producers'
Cooperative, with about 150 families, could not mobilize enough labor to
undertake the execution of these projects. Surplus labor from neighboring
cooperatives could have been borrowed but this would have resulted in
complicated accounting and management problems. The natural thing, therefore, was to expand the surplus labor resource of the production units. A commune with about 5,000 families and 10,000 able-bodied workers is large enough
to handle medium-sized development projects without having to borrow labor
from the outside. The need to make speedy investment in agriculture was also
kept in view at the time of the reorganization of the communes. In the period
1959-1961, relatively less prosperous communes or the communes with serious
problems were separated out to make it easier for the state to channel assistance
(See Appendix: VI,1 and X,1).

Another consideration which led to the formation of the communes was
the desire to make rural areas self-sufficient in all respects. The field of operation of the cooperatives had been found to be limited: their size had worked
as a constraint upon the diversification of their economies. The commune was
a bigger unit which could provide an adequate market for the outlet of small
industries. No wonder, therefore, that the communization of agriculture was
followed by the appearance of a rash of small industries all over the rural
sector. Again, the local cadres took a leap rather than a small step forward.
The mushroom growth of rural industry was checked after 1959; 45 per cent

of the industrial units established in one year after communization were dismantled and the communes were allowed to keep industries for which they themselves could produce raw materials. The dismantling of rural industry alone increased the number of able-bodied workers available to the communes by more than 15 per cent.

The Eight-point Charter.

The communes were formed to implement the following eight-point charter:

1. Construction of water conservancy projects with the help of labor considered surplus to the needs of the agriculture sector.
2. Greater and more scientific use of chemical fertilizer.
3. Adoption of a scientific cropping pattern.
4. Teaching peasants the techniques of deep ploughing and soil amelioration.
5. Increasing yields per acre by resorting to closer planting.
6. Conserving crops by using plant protection material.
7. Greater use of improved farm implements.
8. Better management of farm inputs and outputs.

Communization did help the Chinese to implement an elaborate program of land development, water conservation, and water distribution. In the six years between 1958 and 1964, communes all over China constructed 100 big reservoirs, each with a capacity of over 100 million cubic meters; 100 medium-sized reservoirs with capacities between 10 and 100 million cubic meters, and 50,000 water tanks holding less than 10 million cubic meters. At the same time, these reservoirs have been provided with feed-in and take-out water channels measuring more than 100,000 kilometers in length. This vast system has been provided with electric and diesel pumps producing 4 million horsepower, an increase of more than twelve and a half times over the total pumping power available in 1957.

Mechanization of the Agricultural Sector

A rapid mechanization of the agricultural sector followed communization. The highest rate of increase came in the year 1960-1961, when the total horse-power of all agricultural machinery (pumping stations, mobile water pumps, tractors, threshers, trucks etc.) went up from 1.22 million to 2.23 million (see Table 1 below). Since then the rate of increase has progressively declined. There has, however, been a steady increase in absolute terms.

Table 1

Use of Mechanized Equipment in Chinese Agriculture, 1957-1964

Year	Horsepower of Agricultural Equipment in Use (in millions)	Percentage Rate of Increase
1957	0.56	—
1958	0.69	23.2
1959	0.90	30.4
1960	1.22	36.1
1961	2.23	82.7
1962	3.60	61.4
1963	5.20	44.4
1964	7.00	34.8

The number of pieces of machinery being used in the agricultural sector has also increased considerably; from 11 million in 1957 to 30 million in 1964. The increase here is very much less than the increase in the power generated by them, and this means that the Chinese, over the years, have tended to use more powerful machines (See Table 2). The average horsepower of equipment being used in 1957 was only 0.05. By 1964, this had increased to 0.23, an improvement of almost five times.

6

Table 2

Number of Machines in Use in Chinese Agriculture, 1957-1964

Year	No. of Machines (in millions)	Average Horsepower	Percentage Rate of Increase in No.
1957	11.0	0.05	—
1958	11.8	0.06	7.3
1959	12.9	0.07	9.3
1960	14.8	0.09	14.7
1961	20.9	0.11	40.9
1962	24.7	0.15	18.2
1963	27.8	0.18	12.5
1964	30.0	0.23	7.9

The use of chemical fertilizer is, of course, another index of improvement. The years following communization saw a rapid increase in both production and utilization of chemical fertilizers (See Table 3 below).

Table 3

Production and Utilization of Chemical Fertilizers in Chinese Agriculture,
1954-1964

Year	Amount Produced (in millions of tons)	Rate of Increase (per cent)	Amount Used (in millions of tons)	Rate of Increase (per cent)
1954	0.29	—	0.80	—
1955	0.36	24.2	1.26	57.5
1956	0.62	72.2	1.61	27.8
1957	0.87	41.8	1.94	20.5
1958	1.47	69.0	2.72	40.2
1959	1.78	19.7	2.93	9.9
1960	1.93	8.4	3.67	25.3
1961	1.74	- 9.8	3.54	- 3.6
1962	2.61	50.0	4.22	19.2
1963	3.65	39.1	5.11	21.1
1964	5.66	55.1	6.00	17.4

The Chinese officials attribute the very high rate of increase in land productivity to better water management, increased mechanization, and greater use of chemical fertilizers. Almost nothing is attributed to expansion in area under cultivation. In fact, the entire concentration appears to have been on intensive rather than extensive cultivation. One index of land productivity is output of rice per hectare. Officials of the Ministry of Agriculture gave this to be 1,050 kilograms per hectare in 1949, 1,770 kilograms in 1953, 5,805 kilograms in 1962 and 6,159 kilograms in 1964.

Chapter II

THREE LEVELS OF MANAGEMENT AND OWNERSHIP

China's commune system has "three levels of management and ownership." A commune is usually broken up into ten to twelve production brigades; a production brigade is further subdivided into ten to fifteen production teams. Production assets are owned at all three levels and, as such, all these production units (communes, production brigades, and production teams) can generate income from their own sources. However, in theory as well as in practice, the management at the commune level exercises considerable influence on the management at the levels of production brigades and teams; the leadership at the level of the production brigade, on the other hand, exercises control over that of the production team more in theory than in practice. The system as it has evolved over the years has, therefore, tended to play down the importance of production brigades. In some latter-day communes, for instance, this tier was altogether done away with. For example, the Leap Forward Commune of Inner Mongolia, formed in 1960, has 48 production teams but no brigades. Table 4 below provides similar details about other communes visited by the

Table 4

Organization of the Communes

No.	Commune	No. of Production Brigades.	No. of Production Teams.	Land per Production Team. (hectares)	Workers per Production Team.
1.	Evergreen	12	125	22.4	112.2
2.	Red Star	9	157	71.7	153.3
3.	Leap Forward	—	48	—	7.2
4.	Kawkang	11	59	37.0	67.8
5.	August First	14	73	46.6	60.3
6.	Tsin Yah	7	59	49.9	55.2
7.	Hsin Lung San	20	200	67.4	64.0
8.	Peng Pu	9	101	9.5	84.7
9.	Hsu Hang	11	127	13.1	72.0
10.	West Lake	14	54	6.2	88.9
11.	Tung Chun	10	81	7.3	63.1
12.	People's Suburban	5	26	—	52.5
13.	Stonewell	13	150	20.0	147.8

delegation from Pakistan. All these communes (not counting Leap Forward) have 135 production brigades, or 11.25 production brigades per commune. These production brigades are further subdivided into 1212 production teams, or very nearly 9 production teams per brigade.

The Commune Congress

There is "democratically centralized leadership" at all three levels of management and ownership. The body with most authority, at least in theory, is the Commune Congress with a membership of between 100 and 150. It is an elected body with a term of two years. The electoral college for the congress is formed by production brigade congresses. The electoral system gives proportional representation to groups like peasants, craftsmen, women, youth, minorities, ex-service men and overseas Chinese. Most of the power which rests with the congress is delegated by it to the Commune Management Committee. The members of the committee as well as its director were elected for a two-year term by the congress. The committee has a membership of between 10 and 15.

A quasi-democratic procedure is followed for electing the chief executive of the commune. All those interested in holding the office submit their names to the local county council. The county officials examine the biographical data and antecedents of all the would-be candidates. An approved list of candidates is then sent back to the Commune Congress for final selection. The slate of candidates seldom has a non-cadre represented on it. After approving the names of the candidates, the county council does not put any pressure on the members of the Commune Congress; they are left to vote much as they please.

We were provided with one particularly interesting example of a change in directorship that had been brought about by this democratic process (see Appendix: XI,8). In this case the incumbent, who was defeated by a newcomer, stayed on in the Management Committee as the deputy director (we shall cite below another example of the working of this process). It is possible for a non-cadre to be elected to the directorship of the commune; if that happens,

the person so elected automatically becomes a government cadre. This is why
it is not possible to come across a non-cadre functioning as director of a commune.
For instance, all the thirteen commune directors that we met with were government cadres.

The commune director supervises, with the help of the members of the
Management Committee, the working of the commune secretariat. The secretariat
is organized into a number of departments. The secretariat of Kawkang Commune, for instance, includes the departments of general administration, finance
and accounting, civil affairs (resolution of disputes), education, culture and
public health, people's militia, agricultural production, women's activities,
youth clubs, and workshop management. In this, as in all other communes,
the heads of the administrative departments are taken from the Management
Committee.

The Commune Congress meets once a year primarily to review the work
done by the Management Committee. Sometimes very important decisions
are taken in these meetings. For instance, in 1960, the Congress of Hsu Hang
Commune in the suburb of Shanghai decided to hand over the management
of a vegetable-producing brigade to the Commune Committee. This was done
against the wishes of the director who was then dropped from the Management
Committee.

Every two years, the Commune Congress also elects a Supervisory Committee which draws its entire membership of between twenty to twenty-five
from the Communist Party. The main function of this committee is to insure
that the policies laid down by the Communist Party are faithfully and dutifully
carried out by the Commune Management Committee. No duplication is allowed
in the membership of the two committees.

The Congress-Supervisory Committee-Management Committee apparatus
exists at the level of the production brigades as well. The Production Brigade
Congress has a membership of about fifty and is elected once every year by
the production team congresses. The Brigade Congress elects every year a
Management Committee and its director who is usually not a cadre. (Only very

large production brigades have cadres as their directors. For instance, six of the thirteen production brigades of Stonewell Commune have cadre-directors.) The Supervisory Committee, also elected by the Brigade Congress, has a term of one year. As for the communes, all members of the Supervisory Committee belong to the Communist Party.

All the able-bodied workers of a production team automatically become the members of the Production Team Congress. Every year the congress elects a Management Committee (seven to ten members) and a Production Team Leader. There is, however, no Supervisory Committee at the level of the production teams. Since 1961, the production team congresses have been electing one supervisor to oversee the work of the Management Committee.

All the land, cultivated or not cultivated, is owned by the commune. It may not, however, be directly managed by its management committee. For management purposes, it may be leased out either to production brigades or to production teams. This division of responsibility between ownership and management gives the Commune Management Committee the power of overseeing the work of other production units. The commune management, therefore, can and sometimes does order production units to make important changes in the way the leased-out land is being used.

Sources of Income

The production units do not make any payments to the commune for using land leased out to them. The Commune Management Committee has, therefore, to look for other sources of income. Ownership of machinery and equipment provides it with one important source. Tractors, threshers, trucks, and pumping stations are more often than not owned by the commune. These are rented out to production units. Maintenance of the rented machinery is the responsibility of the production units. However, repair workshops are owned by the communes and the production units have to pay for getting their equipment repaired in them.

In 1964, the Peng Pu Commune Tractor and Agriculture Implement Repair Station contributed ¥7,531 to the income of the commune. Small industrial enterprises are another source of income for the communes. The share of industry in the total income of the communes declined considerably after 1961. Some important industrial units have remained even after the reorganization of communal economy in the period 1959-1961. These contribute substantial additional income to the communes. Red Star Commune of Peking is still operating a wrapping-paper plant. The plant employs 520 workers and yields an income of about ¥250,000 every year. Brick-making, straw mat-weaving, rice-husking, and grain-milling are some of the favorite forms of industrial activity at the commune level. The third important source of commune income is the ownership of specialized production brigades. Many communes have production brigades engaged in such specialized activities as producing vegetables in hothouses, growing fruits, honey bee-keeping, etc. These brigades are usually directly managed by the commune directorate. A fourth source of income for the commune is the share that they receive from the reserve and welfare funds managed by the lower production units. Amounts thus received from the production units can be used only for specific purposes (See Chapter IV).

Very few production brigades have independent sources of income. The production brigade was an important level of ownership and management in the earlier communes. These communes were very big; many had more than 150 production teams in their control. In their case, it was essential to have an intermediate tier between the commune and production team levels. With the breakup of the bigger communes in the period 1959-1961, production brigades automatically ceased to function as effective units of production and management. Production brigades continue to retain their importance in the areas where the communes, for one reason or another, were not reorganized. Production brigades in Hsin Lung San Commune, which has 200 teams, and in Stonewell Commune, which has 150 teams, continue to perform important management and production functions. Stonewell Commune is the only example we saw of a commune being enlarged in size as a result of the 1959-1961 reorganization program. This was done in order to operate more effectively the water drainage and irrigation system that was being installed in this area. Here the Commune Management Committee had delegated most of its powers to the brigade management committees. It is no wonder, therefore, that six of the thirteen brigades have government cadres as directors of their management committees.

The bulk of the communes' agricultural income accrues to the production teams. The teams are entitled to manage themselves the returns they receive from the lands they cultivate. That is why they are called "basic units of accounting in the commune system." By management of returns is meant the distribution among the workers who produce it, the government, the reserve fund, the welfare fund, and a fund established for meeting future (next year's) production costs (see Chapter III). The teams, however, have to manage their resources according to the principles laid down by the state and in conformity to the wishes of the commune leaders. The latter can and often do exercise considerable influence on the decisions of the production team leaders. The communes can exert pressure on the production teams for two reasons. We have already seen that the commune management is made up almost totally of cadres who, because of their official status and close connection with government bureaucracy and party leadership, wield tremendous power. The production team draws its leadership from the peasants who are easily awed by the position and status of the cadres. Also, as we saw above, communes have large financial resources at their disposal which are given to the production teams for capital investment purposes. It would naturally be very difficult for truant teams to claim these resources. In matters of distribution of funds for development purposes, the commune cadres seem to have the final say and the production team cannot hope for any intervention from above (county or province). While the management of production resources within the commune hierarchy was considerably decentralized in the period 1959-1961, it does not seem right to read into this development a process of a total disintegration of the system.

14

State Control

The Communist state exercises direct as well as indirect control of the communes. An elaborate government machinery exists to supervise the working of the communes, to render advice to the commune level cadres, to coordinate the development plans of the communes, and to provide financial and technical assistance to relatively backward production units. The Department of People's Communes' Affairs in the Ministry of Agriculture in Peking is one of the fourteen departments into which the Ministry is divided. (The other thirteen are: General Administration, Agricultural Science and Technology, Agricultural Education and Propaganda, Agricultural Finance and Capital Construction, Animal Husbandry and Fisheries, Land Improvement and Soil Amelioration, Plant Protection, Disease Control and Insecticides, Fertilizer Production, Distribution and Procurement, Industrial Crops, Oil-bearing Crops, Food-Grains, Foreign Trade and Foreign Relations, and Political Work.) All provincial agricultural departments also have "commune affairs offices". The county governments have "commune management sections" as well. A parallel exists under the Bureau of Commune Management located at Peking. There are bureaus in all the provinces and counties. However, there is no duplication between the working of the department-office-section under the Ministry of Agriculture and that under the Bureau of Commune Management. The former is concerned only with insuring that the development plans drawn up by the communes are in keeping with its own overall agricultural development program. On the other hand, the latter organization is concerned with supervising the day-to-day working of the communes. The bureau, therefore, works as the field-arm of the Ministry. The plans drawn up by the Ministry are based on the data supplied by the bureau; once the plans have been forwarded, it is the business of the bureau to break them down according to provinces, counties and communes. The plan that is eventually handed down to the communes is in the form of production targets. The communes are left to devise the programs for achieving these targets themselves. The programs so drawn up are submitted by the communes to the county governments for purposes of scrutiny and approval.

The commune management, therefore, comes in touch, for the most part, with the administrations at the county level. All the counties have an elaborate organization to maintain close liaison with the communes in their areas. For instance, Tsin Yah Commune of Changchun is controlled by a county council whose department of agriculture is divided into several sections. The section responsible for commune affairs has 23 personnel, 13 of whom are agro-technicians, and 10 administrators. The section looks after 11 communes, 100 production brigades, and 1000 production teams. It receives annual development programs from all the communes at least three months before they are launched. It is also provided with a monthly statement of accounts from every commune. The commune cadres are encouraged to keep themselves in close touch with the section officials; the officials themselves visit all the communes at least once every six months.

The cadres exercise indirect control on the working of the communes. The number of cadres working in a particular commune depends upon its size and income. Peng Pu Commune of Shanghai, with a gross income of 3.862 million yuan has thirteen cadres working in various capacities. People's Suburban Commune of Kiangsu Province has been given only six cadres, but then it has a gross income of only ¥1.1 million. Cadres are appointed by the county councils but usually belong to the communes in which they work. They are, therefore, seldom transferred from one commune to another. Nine of the thirteen communes that we visited had cadre-directors who had been appointed immediately after the formation of the communes.

Cadres in the Communes

Cadres are paid by the state but have to spend at least sixty working days in the field along with the ordinary members of the commune. The average salary of a commune level cadre is ¥60.6 per month which is, as we shall see below, slightly less than twice the amount earned by an average able-bodied worker in the Chinese agricultural sector. The directors of production brigades and leaders of production teams do not receive their salaries from the government.

They have to work on the land like ordinary peasants. Most brigades and teams, however, subsidize the incomes of their leaders to bring them to the level of the income of an average worker. The leader of Mei Chi Hwu Production Brigade of West Lake Commune of Chekiang Province was able to put in enough work in the field in 1964 to receive ¥ 26.0 from income distributed among the workers by his management committee. However, the leader had spent several days out of the village trying to secure funds from the local branch of the Agricultural Bank for the construction of a pumping station. The management committee, accordingly, allowed a subsidy of ¥ 11.0 to be paid out to him every month. The subsidy is given to the leaders out of the production team's "production costs" in recognition of the fact that these officials cannot spend enough time in the field to earn the same number of "work points" as other able-bodied workers.

It is, therefore, in a rigid framework of direct and indirect control that the "decentralized democratic system of leadership and management" works in the communes. However, this does not mean that decentralization of operation has been achieved only on paper. For, despite the controls described above, the commune managements and leaders of the production units are able to make important decisions on their own.

Chapter III

GENERATION OF INCOME AND ITS DISTRIBUTION

The analysis presented in this chapter is based mostly on the data collected from the thirteen communes visited by the delegation. This data has to be handled with caution for at least three important reasons. First, a sample of thirteen communes can hardly be used with confidence in drawing general conclusions. Four of the thirteen communes would, most probably, not figure in a randomly drawn sample; two of them (Evergreen and Red Star Communes of Peking municipality) are obviously showpieces, shown to most foreigners; one of them (Leap Forward Commune in Inner Mongolia) belongs to a relatively underdeveloped region of the country, has organizational aspects not shared by other communes in China, and is concerned almost totally with animal husbandry; and the fourth (People's Suburban Commune of Kiangsu province) is a highly specialized commune, deriving one hundred per cent of its income from fishing. For this reason, in most of this section of the study, we shall not be using data obtained from the Inner Mongolia and Kiangsu communes. At times we shall drop Evergreen and Red Star communes from our analysis in order to obtain more meaningful conclusions for Chinese agriculture. Second, time series data for a commune may not refer to the same geographical units. We have already seen that many changes were made in the boundaries of the communes in the period 1959-1961. This fact may have been ignored by the commune management at the time of the presentation of data to the delegation. Third, our sample narrows even further when we discuss important matters like the rate of increase in the use of chemical fertilizer or the pattern of distribution of production costs. This happens because the commune cadres did not present data according to any unified pattern. Some cadres were able to provide more information than others.

Our caution about the smallness of the sample is highlighted by the tremendous differences in size, composition, etc. (see Table 5) among the communes.

Table 5

Area Cultivated and Population of Communes Visited

No.	Commune	Province	Cultivated land (hectares)	Number of Families	Number of workers	Workers per hectare
1.	Evergreen	Peking	2,805	8,100	14,000	4.99
2.	Red Star	Peking	11,251	11,000	24,000	2.13
3.	Leap Forward	Inner Mongolia	–	252	350	–
4.	Kawkang	Liaoning	2,183	2,988	4,000	1.83
5.	August First	Liaoning	3,401	2,800	4,400	1.29
6.	Tsin Yah	Kirin	4,329	3,000	4,800	1.11
7.	Hsin Lung San	Kirin	13,528	10,130	12,790	0.95
8.	Peng Pu	Shanghai	958	3,721	8,552	8.93
9.	Hsu Hang	Shanghai	1,664	4,629	9,149	5.50
10.	West Lake	Chekiang	333	1,800	4,800	14.41
11.	Tung Chun	Chekiang	588	2,014	5,112	8.69
12.	Peoples Suburban	Kiangsu	–	553	1,365	–
13.	Stonewell	Kwangtung	3,000	11,900	22,000	7.33

The System of Accounting

All production units (communes, brigades, teams) follow the same system of accounting. Uniformity is further insured by the use of the same or very similar account books all over the country. The income of the production unit is entered in the account book in gross terms; various items of expenditure are grouped together under five main headings. The first charge on the gross income of a production unit is agricultural tax. In addition to this, there are two more obligatory charges on gross income: contributions made by the production units into the reserve and welfare funds. A production unit is also expected to set aside a portion of its current income for meeting future (usually only the subsequent year's) production costs. What remains after all these deductions have been made is distributed among all the able-bodied workers listed in the production units employment ledger. "Distributed income" or "net income," as this last item is called, is, therefore, a residual item.

Deductions from the gross income, under the five items listed above, are made by the production unit managers according to a very broad formula laid down by the government in 1961. The production units, apart from meeting fully the obligation of the state, are obliged to contribute at least 10 per cent of their incomes into the reserve fund and 2 per cent into the welfare fund. It is also mandatory for them to distribute at least 50 per cent among their able-bodied members.

The production team leaders may, on the receipt of permission from the county administration, deviate from the state's prescribed formula. The following can be advanced as legitimate reasons. First, exceptionally poor production units may contribute less than 10 per cent to the reserve fund in order to distribute a greater proportion of income among their workers. In their case the state undertakes to provide funds for development schemes. Second, relatively more prosperous production units may distribute less than 50 per cent among their workers. In their case the state insists that payments of savings so made be put into the reserve or welfare funds. Third, during emergencies, the production units may not set aside any amount for meeting anticipated production costs during the following year. In such contingencies, the Agricultural Bank of China advances short term, low interest loans to cover the outlay on production costs. County administrators all over China seem to have been fairly liberal in granting production units permission to deviate from the distribution formula. This is indicated by the statistics furnished by the Bureau of Commune Management in Peking. (See Table 6 below.) According to this, the agricultural

Table 6

Distribution of Gross Agricultural Income in China, 1964

	Item	Percentage of Gross Income
(i)	Agriculture Tax	7.0
(ii)	Reserve Fund	10.0
(iii)	Welfare Fund	3.0
(iv)	Production Cost	25.0
(v)	Distributed Income	55.0
	Total	100.0

workers in China in 1964 received 5 per cent more income than had been actually stipulated by the state. The total contributions to the welfare funds were also a percentage point higher.

Table 7 gives an income distributional breakdown for all the thirteen communes visited by the delegation. As was perhaps to be expected, there are considerable differences in the proportions of gross incomes set aside by different communes for different purposes.

Table 7

Distribution of Gross Income in the Thirteen Communes, 1964.

No.	Commune	Gross Income (G.I.)	Agriculture Tax		Reserve Fund		Welfare Fund		Production Cost		Distributed Income	
			Amount	% of G.I.	Amount	% of G.I.	Amount	% of G.I.	Amount	% of G.I.	Amount	% of G.I.
1.	Evergreen	13.300	0.399	3.0	1.590	12.0	0.133	1.1	4.520	34.0	6.650	50.0
2.	Red Star	27.000	1.700	6.3	4.100	15.2	1.400	5.2	6.200	23.0	13.600	50.4
3.	Leap Forward	0.250	0.010	4.0	0.025	10.0	0.008	3.0	0.033	13.0	0.175	70.0
4.	Kawkang	2.202	0.111	5.1	0.178	8.0	0.051	2.3	0.660	30.1	1.211	54.5
5.	August First	3.900	0.200	5.1	0.660	16.9	0.200	5.1	0.780	20.0	2.060	52.8
6.	Tsin Yah	2.250	0.100	4.4	0.180	8.0	0.050	2.2	0.673	29.9	1.247	55.4
7.	Hsin Lung San	6.600	0.530	8.0	0.330	5.0	0.130	2.0	1.650	25.0	3.960	60.6
8.	Peng Pu	3.862	0.250	6.5	0.480	12.4	0.070	1.8	0.859	22.2	2.203	57.0
9.	Hsu Hang	4.250	0.220	5.2	0.390	9.2	0.153	3.6	1.150	27.0	2.340	55.1
10.	West Lake	1.760	0.170	6.1	0.112	6.4	0.018	1.0	0.333	18.9	1.190	67.6
11.	Tung Chun	1.320	0.066	5.0	0.092	7.0	0.026	2.0	0.286	21.7	0.850	64.4
12.	People's Suburban	1.100	0.006	0.5	0.110	10.0	0.028	2.5	0.187	17.0	0.770	70.0
13.	Stonewell	9.000	0.360	4.0	0.450	5.0	0.090	1.0	2.700	30.0	5.400	60.0
	Total	76.794	4.122	5.4	8.697	11.3	2.357	3.1	20.031	26.0	41.656	54.2

Agricultural Tax

The collection of tax from the agricultural sector was first systematized by the state in 1953. A simple formula was adopted. Almost all the cooperatives (those exempted or charged at lower rates were the very poor ones) were ordered to pay 10 per cent of their gross income to the state as a tax on agriculture. Tax assessment was to be made at the beginning of every year; in this way the state reserved for itself the right to claim subsequently any proportion of the gross agricultural income. In 1954, however, the government took the important decision to fix the level of agricultural tax in perpetuity. In the future the cooperatives were to pay the same amount in money terms as they had actually paid in 1953. Some adjustments were made; those cooperatives which had had exceptionally good output in 1953 had their assessments scaled down by a little. By adopting this form of assessment, the government provided the cooperatives with a positive incentive to develop their resources and increase their incomes. As the government claimed nothing out of the increases in incomes registered in the period 1953-1958, variations in the incidence of taxation in 1958 ranged between 7.4 per cent to 10.3 per cent of the gross incomes of the cooperatives.

In 1958, at the time of communization of agriculture, the government did not adopt a new formula of assessing agricultural tax. The government specified that the communes, over the years, would pay to the state the sum of the amounts the federating cooperatives would have paid had they continued to exist independently. Some adjustments were made following the reorganization of the communes in 1959-1961.

That the proportion of the gross income paid to the government in 1964 as agricultural tax can serve as an indicator of the rate of growth of agricultural incomes is borne out by the data presented in Table 8 below. In 1964, Hsin

Table 8

Growth in Incomes and Agricultural Tax as Percentage of Gross
Incomes of Evergreen and Hsin Lung San Communes, 1958-1964

Year	EVERGREEN				HSIN LUNG SAN			
	Gross Income (millions)	Rate of Increase, %	Ag. Tax	Ag. Tax as % of Income	Gross Income (millions)	Rate of Increase, %	Ag. Tax	Ag. Tax as % of Income
1958	5.32	—	0.399	7.5	5.29	—	0.53	10.0
1959	6.07	14.0	0.399	6.6	5.32	0.6	0.53	9.9
1960	6.94	14.3	0.399	6.2	5.01	- 5.8	0.53	10.6
1961	7.74	11.5	0.399	5.2	4.92	- 1.8	0.53	10.8
1962	9.32	22.1	0.399	4.3	5.24	6.5	0.53	10.1
1963	12.01	28.8	0.399	3.3	6.21	18.5	0.53	8.5
1964	13.30	10.8	0.399	3.0	6.60	6.3	0.53	8.0

Lung San Commune of Kirin province was paying more tax in absolute terms as compared with Evergreen Commune of Peking, although the former had a gross income almost exactly half that of the latter. In 1958, at the time of their formation, the two communes had almost the same incomes. Even then, Hsin Lung San paid a larger proportion of agricultural tax than Evergreen. (These figures indicate that the growth patterns in the two communes were established even before their formation.) By 1964, this difference had widened even further.

Reserve Fund

The contribution to the reserve fund is the second charge on the income of the production units. These funds are operated separately by the communes and production teams. The accumulation of resources at the commune level is usually employed for financing the development projects of those production teams that cannot afford to execute them without outside assistance. Some communes also use their reserves for creating facilities like repair shops, cold storages, hothouses, etc. In this way the commune is able to add to its income-generating capacity.

The main purpose for making production units contribute at least a tenth of their gross incomes to the reserve funds is to make it possible for them to execute development schemes financed largely from their own resources. In Chapter II, we got a general idea of the type of development activity that have been undertaken by the communes in their areas. In the Appendix, we have provided details of the types of work done by the thirteen communes we visited.

The data of Table 7 are in aggregative terms; they provide figures for total contributions made by all the production units within the communes. Data in Table 9 give some idea of the breakdown of contributions to the reserve fund between the commune itself and its production teams. In the period 1959-1964, all the production units in Hsu Hang made a total contribution of ¥1.94 million to the reserve fund. Out of this, ¥1.375 million, or 70.9%

Table 9

Breakdown of Contributions to the Reserve Fund in Hsu Hang Commune, 1959-1964

Year	Gross Income (in millions)					Contribution to Reserve Fund (in millions)					Expenditure (in millions)	
	Total for the Commune	Prod. Teams	Comm. Enterprises	2 as % of 1	3 as % of 1	Total	By Comm. Enterprises	By Prod. Teams	7 as % of 6	8 as % of 6	Cumulative	11 as % of 1
	1	2	3	4	5	6	7	8	9	10	11	12
1959	3.100	1.600	1.500	51.6	48.4	0.300	0.210	0.090	70.0	30.0	0.280	90.3
1960	2.570	1.090	1.480	42.4	57.6	0.250	0.175	0.075	70.0	30.0	0.400	72.6
1961	2.804	1.304	1.500	46.4	53.4	0.300	0.220	0.080	73.3	26.7	0.405	52.9
1962	3.300	1.650	1.650	50.0	50.0	0.325	0.225	0.100	69.2	31.8	0.419	35.6
1963	3.810	2.040	1.770	53.5	46.5	0.375	0.275	0.100	73.3	26.7	0.442	27.9
1964	4.250	2.280	1.970	53.6	46.4	0.390	0.270	0.120	69.2	30.8	0.530	27.3
1959-64	19.834	9.964	9.870	50.3	49.7	1.940	1.375	0.565	70.9	29.1	0.530	27.3

of the total was contributed by the commune from the income earned from its own enterprises. The main source of income for the commune is a production brigade that specializes in producing vegetables. The production teams also pay the commune management to have their implements repaired in the central workshop. By 1964, the commune had spent only 530,000 yuan, or 27.3 per cent of the total accumulated reserves for development purposes. If this pattern is repeated in all the other Chinese communes, it is easy to see why the commune management exercises so much control over the leadership of the production teams.

While the commune managements discourage production teams from saving less than 10 per cent of their incomes for development purposes, the teams are allowed to save more if they can afford to do so. For instance, in 1964 all the production units of Tsin Yah Commune together saved 8 per cent of their total income for this purpose, but Chao Tien Production Team was able to set aside as much as 15 per cent. In 1964 this team exhausted all its reserves by purchasing a grain milling machine. Over the years, the same team has been able to buy six low-lift pumps, three hand carts, and two hand-power tillers.

Welfare Fund

Welfare funds are also operated separately by all the production units within a commune. Accumulations in the funds are used for a variety of purposes. Expenditures are made on meeting the current and not the capital costs of welfare projects undertaken by the production units. The production units of Peng Pu Commune of Shanghai and Stonewell Commune of Kwangtung contributed a total amount of ¥160,000 to the welfare funds. Out of this ¥158,000 were spent by the two communes on various welfare activities, as detailed in Table 10 below. In Stonewell Commune the expenditure exceeded the total contributions made to the fund by ¥11,000. This difference was made up by borrowing ¥6,000 from the savings made in the past and ¥5,000 from the Credit Cooperative Society. The latter has lent ¥22,000 to the commune for welfare activities in the period 1958-1964.

Table 10

Expenditures on Welfare Activities in Peng Pu
and Stonewell Communes, 1964

No.	Item of Expenditure	PENG PU		STONEWELL	
		Expenditure (yuan)	% of total	Expenditure (yuan)	% of total
1.	Relief to poor families	52,000	74.3	74,000	73.3
2.	School feeding	9,000	12.9	13,000	12.9
3.	Food for patients	7,000	10.0	3,000	2.8
4.	Reading Room supplies	1,000	1.4	—	—
5.	Sports	1,000	1.4	—	—
6.	Community Dining Rooms	—	—	1,000	0.1
7.	Poor People's Home	—	—	10,000	10.0
	Total	70,000	100.0	101,000	100.0

As we see from the table, the bulk of the expenditure is in the form of relief payments made to poor families. A family qualifies as "poor" for two reasons: first, it may have a very low worker to non-worker ratio; second, its able-bodied workers may not be able to accumulate enough work points to afford a decent living to the members. In Peng Pu Commune, the non-worker to worker ratio is 2.3 (see Table 5), which means that an able-bodied worker here supports, apart from himself, on the average, 1.3 non-workers. In this commune, a family with a ratio of 3.5 qualifies for support from the welfare fund. A typical family supported by the fund would be made up of two workers (husband and wife), six children, and an old person. Peng Pu production units were providing this type of relief to 213 families. In 1964 a poor family received, on the average, ¥244 per year.

Production Costs

Included in production costs are all those agricultural inputs which a production unit has to purchase from the outside. Thus, if a production team itself grows all the fodder needed for its animals, then expenditure on fodder would not figure under production costs. Figures of Table 7, therefore, do not give the real cost of inputs used by the various communes. There is no way of gauging the extent of underestimation involved. Items that tend to get excluded include animal fodder, seeds, and farm manure.

Table 11 provides a breakdown of production costs for all communes in China. These data were supplied by the Bureau of Commune Management. Table 12 supplies the same breakdown for those communes visited by the delegation.

Seed, fuel, power, chemical fertilizer and insecticides are obtained by the commune management from various state trading corporations and distributed to the production teams. For these inputs the state charges the same price for most of China. For instance the price charged for a ton of ammonium sulphate all over China in 1965 was ¥340.0 and electric power for electric pumps was being sold at 7 cents per kwh. Animal feed is either grown by the production teams themselves or purchased from neighboring teams that happen

Table 11

Breakdown of Production Costs for all Chinese Communes, 1964

No.	Item	Expenditure as percentage of total production cost
1.	Seed	18.0
2.	Animal Feed	35.0
3.	Chemical Fertilizer and Insecticides	10.4
4.	Tractor Ploughing Charges	2.8
5.	Electricity Charges	0.8
6.	Fuel for Transportation	2.0
7.	Maintenance of Trucks and Carts	11.0
8.	Maintenance of Implements	13.0
9.	Miscellaneous	7.0
	Total	100.0

Table 12

Breakdown of Production Costs in Peng Pu, Tsin Yah,
and West Lake Communes, 1964.

No.	Item of expenditure	Peng Pu Cost (yuan)	% of total	Tsin Yah Cost (yuan)	% of total	West Lake Cost (yuan)	% of total
1.	Seed	194,700	22.7	150,000	22.3	74,000	22.2
2.	Animal Feed	320,000	37.3	290,000	43.1	1,200	0.4
3.	Fertilizer	151,000	17.6	85,000	12.6	119,880	36.0
4.	Tractor Ploughing	9,250	1.1	30,000)	4.5)	–	–
5.	Electricity	2,400	0.3	)	)	680	0.2
6.	Fuel	4,500	0.5	)	)	1,400	0.4
7.	Workshop Charges	14,490	1.7	17,200	2.6	8,900	2.7
8.	Miscellaneous	162,110	18.9	100,800	15.0	126,940	38.1
	Total	859,000	100.0	673,000	100.0	330,000	100.0

to have a surplus. We saw considerable evidence of this type of trading between the production teams within the same commune. Trucks, tractors, threshers, etc., are generally owned by the commune and hired out to the production teams at the rentals fixed by the Commune Management Committee. Workshops for repairing farm implements are also owned by the communes. For instance, the Evergreen Commune workshop had ten lathes and employed 110 workers. The net income from this workshop was more than 80,000 yuan.

In Peng Pu and Tsin Yah Communes, expenditure on animal feed was even higher than the national average of 35 per cent; in West Lake Commune it was considerably smaller. An outstanding item of expenditure in West Lake Commune was fertilizer. In China (see Chapter V) according to the official view, the use of fertilizer for specialized production (vegetables, fruits, tea, etc.) has been encouraged even when this was at the expense of food grain production.

Personal Incomes

What is left from the gross income after making all these deductions is distributed among the able-bodied workers of a production unit. On the average, 50 per cent of peasant wages are paid in grain and 50 per cent in cash. Wages are paid on the basis of "work points" allotted to a worker by the production team and the number of work days he puts in in a year. Work points are allotted on the basis of a worker's ability to do work in the field and his general attitude toward manual labor. Thus eight hours of work may entitle one worker to ten points while another, for the same number of hours in the field, may get only six points. If a worker puts in less than eight hours of work on a particular day, his work points for that day are correspondingly reduced. Points are allotted at the beginning of every month in an open meeting in which all the peasants participate enthusiastically. We attended one such meeting in which the final formula was accepted by all the members of the production team after what appeared to be at times a fairly heated debate. At the end of the agricultural year, the net income of the production unit is calculated by making all the deductions mentioned above; the residual is then divided by the total number of points obtained by all the members. This calculation determines the money value of a work point. The yearly wage of the workers is determined by multiplying the value of the work point with the number of points obtained by each one of them over the year.

In 1964, the average wage received by the workers in the thirteen communes was ¥388.5. This is reduced to only ¥272 if we exclude the not very typical communes of Evergreen, Red Star, Leap Forward and People's Suburban. The Bureau of Communes' figure for the average agricultural wage in China in 1964 was ¥408. Able-bodied workers in our typical communes seem to have earned one-third less than typical workers in Chinese agriculture. The following factors may be responsible for this difference: first, our figures do not include incomes earned from private plots. The bureau's figures may not only include these but may also incorporate incomes from subsidiary occupations like handicrafts, etc. Second, only 50 per cent of the wages are paid in cash, the rest is received by the workers in kind. The money value of the agricultural wage, therefore, depends on the prices at which distributed food grains, etc., are valued. There is a difference in the price that the state pays to the production units for their agricultural produce and what it charges itself from the communes. Valuation of wages in kind at these two different prices would naturally lead to an overestimation by the state. Third, we have calculated average wages by simply dividing the total distributed income by the number of able-bodied workers. No transfer payments (payments to poor families out of the welfare fund) have been included. The government figure may also incorporate these.

Of the thirteen communes visited by us, only five (Evergreen, Red Star, August First, Leap Forward and People's Suburban) had paid out higher than average national wages to their able-bodied workers. In this group of five, we can identify two different communes: the very rich ones (Evergreen, Red Star and August First) and the very poor ones (Leap Forward and People's Suburban). The latter group had achieved higher wages for its workers by distributing to them 70 per cent of their gross income (Table 7). The former

Table 13

Family Income and Agricultural Wages in the Thirteen Communes, 1964

| | | | FAMILIES | | WORKERS | |
No.	Communes	Net Income Distributed (¥ million)	Number	Received income per family(yuan)	Number	Received Income per worker(yuan)
1.	Evergreen	6.650	8,100	821.0	14,000	475.0
2.	Red Star	13.600	11,000	1236.4	24,000	567.6
3.	Leap Forward	0.175	252	694.4	350	500.0
4.	Kawkang	1.211	2,988	405.3	4,000	302.8
5.	August First	2.060	2,800	735.7	4,400	468.2
6.	Tsin Yah	1.247	3,000	415.6	4,800	259.8
7.	Hsin Lung San	3.960	10,130	390.9	12,790	309.6
8.	Peng Pu	2.203	3,721	592.0	8,552	257.6
9.	Hsu Hang	2.340	4,649	503.3	9,149	255.8
10.	West Lake	1.190	1,800	661.1	4,800	247.9
11.	Tung Chun	0.850	2,014	422.1	5,112	166.3
12.	People's Suburban	0.770	553	1392.4	1,365	564.1
13.	Stonewell	5.400	11,900	453.8	22,000	245.5
	TOTAL	41.656	62,907	662.2	115,318	361.2

group had achieved a higher standard of living for its workers in spite of the fact that only half of the gross income was given out as wages. In fact, the percentage of gross income distributed to the able-bodied workers of Evergreen, Red Star and August First Communes was less than that for any other commune visited by us. This result appears to have been deliberately achieved; the most likely and probable aim being to reduce the gap between the distributed income per worker in rich and poor communes. The average distributed income per able-bodied worker in Evergreen, Red Star and August First Commune was ¥526.2 in 1964. The average for the remaining communes, not counting Leap Forward and People's Suburban Communes, was only ¥264.2. This gap appeared despite different rates of distributing incomes adopted by the rich and poor communes. Thus the three richer communes distributed to their workers 50.5 per cent of their gross income while the remaining communes distributed as much as 58.5 per cent. Had the comparatively richer communes also distributed their gross incomes in the same proportion as the others, the received income per worker for them would have been ¥609.4. This would have increased the income gap to ¥354.2. Or, conversely, had the poorer communes adopted the same distribution pattern as the richer ones, income per worker in their case would have been reduced to ¥228.2, making the income gap equal to ¥298.0.

Despite the effort to equalize wages, a wide income differential exists in Chinese agriculture. For instance, the workers of the Red Star Commune of Peking received wages almost two-and-a half times those received by workers of Chekiang's Tung Chun Commune. The agricultural wage of Red Star Commune workers was 39.2 per cent higher than the national average; that of an average worker in Tung Chun Commune was less than two-fifths. This disparity is somewhat reduced if we remove the non-typical communes from this part of the analysis. Even then, the wages of workers in the August First Commune were 187 per cent higher than those in Tung Chun Commune.

Some idea of regional disparities can be had from Table 14. As is to be expected, high population areas have lower incomes per able-bodied worker. Thus as we move down from the northeastern provinces of Kirin and Liaoning toward the southeastern province of Kwangtung, there is a steady decline

Table 14

Agricultural Wages Received per Month by Able-Bodied Workers
in Eight Chinese Provinces, 1964
(yuan)

1. Peking	44.41
2. Inner Mongolia	47.22
3. Liaoning	32.45
4. Kirin	24.66
5. Shanghai	21.39
6. Chekiang	17.15
7. Kiangsu	47.00
8. Kwangtung	18.75

Note: Wages per worker have been calculated by taking weighted averages of the communes visited in the areas.

in the income of agricultural workers. Kiangsu province appears to present an exception. In this province, however, the delegation visited only one commune and that too was engaged in fishing. In order to pull its population out of desperate poverty, the Commune Management Committee was distributing 70 per cent of its gross earnings as wages. The figure of ¥47.00 as monthly wage is, therefore, not representative of the area.

The Chinese communes have declared that their policy is to remove this difference as rapidly as possible. The government expects to achieve equality in the following ways. First, by providing state assistance to the relatively less developed regions of the country. Second, by identifying really poor production units, scientifically determining the reasons for their poverty, and trying to solve their peculiar problems by giving them massive financial and technical assistance. "Identification and separation" of poor production units has been done at two different levels. Every county has a few backward areas; if geographically contiguous and large enough (in population or area), they have been formed into communes, earmarked for special treatment. Similarly, poorer production teams within the communes have also been set aside for special attention. In fact. at the time of the reorganization of the communes, the poverty factor was constantly kept in view by the county officials. (For an example, see Appendix: VI, 1, 7.)

Third, by diversifying the economies of the poorer production brigades. By "diversification," the Chinese no longer mean the adoption of a mixed agricultural-industrial economy by the communes. Having tried this in 1958 and failed, the Chinese have turned to another form of diversification–"production spread to be achieved within the agricultural sector." The purely grain-growing areas are being encouraged to grow fruits, vegetables, medicinal herbs, etc. In order to encourage this type of "production-spread," the Chinese press gives prominence to success stories in which the turning point came when the production units partially switched from traditional to non-traditional crops. Under the pricing policy followed at present by the government, there is no doubt that the communes going in for "special crops" stand to earn a good deal more than those that only produce food grains. In Chekiang province, for instance, the West Lake Commune, which derives 80 per cent of its gross income from tea, is able to distribute 50 per cent more wages to its workers than Tung Chun Commune which grows mostly food grains.

Fourth, to adopt a labor policy which makes the industrial sector depend largely on hands recruited from the poorer regions. Such a policy, it is hoped, would reduce the pressure of population in the relatively less developed regions of the country. The officials are, however, aware that this policy can remove from these areas their only economically important asset, able-bodied workers. A lowered man-to-land ratio in which the composition of population has changed in favor of the very old and the very young cannot be regarded as an improvement. It is to prevent this sort of thing from happening that the leadership within a production unit has a strict control on labor migration.

Agricultural Bank of China

As we can see, this four-point program calls for a massive government participation in the development of backward areas. The flow of financial assistance to the communes was systematized in 1963 with the creation of the Agricultural Bank of China. The bank is concerned mainly with the development of the poorer regions; relatively more advanced regions have sometimes received support when the projects for which aid is being sought involve outlays well beyond the resources of the sponsoring production unit.

Development loans to the communes are given in two ways: advances are either made through the Commune Credit Cooperative Society or directly to the production unit which is in need of financial assistance. The commune credit cooperative societies usually ask for financial assistance from the bank without specifying the exact purpose of the loans. All that the bank insures is that the borrowing credit cooperative society has the wherewithal to meet its financial obligations in the future. However, a production unit making a direct application to the bank has to follow strictly the following procedure: first, the project for which help is being sought has to be a part of the county development program. (The county development program is formulated by dovetailing the outlay and output targets received by it from the provincial government with the development schemes suggested by the communes.) Second, the project has to be specifically approved by the county government. Third, the project must be fully planned. This means that the application for assistance must be accompanied by project blueprints, cost estimates, estimates of returns, and estimate of time needed to implement the project. The bank advances two types of loans: long term and short term. Long term loans, repayable over a period of three to five years, carry a simple rate of interest of 0.18 per cent per month. These loans are meant to be used to implement water conservancy, land drainage, soil improvement, and multi-purpose irrigation projects. They can also be used for purchasing big and small agricultural implements. Short-term loans have periods of maturation of between twelve to eighteen months. They carry a rate of interest of 6 per cent per month and are usually advanced to meet current production costs such as the purchase of farm manure, animal feed, seeds, fertilizer, and insecticides.

The impression we gathered from our visit to the various communes was that only 5 to 10 per cent of the total development costs was met by outside help. According to officials of the Agricultural Bank of China, however, the commune reserve funds have accounted for only 80 per cent of the total outlay on various types of development projects completed in the period 1953-1964. The remaining 20 per cent of the total cost was financed out of the loans advanced by the bank. In the two years since it started operating, the bank has made total advances of ¥200 million for development purposes. This means that the total expenditure on development schemes executed by the communes in 1963 and 1964 was ¥1,000 million.

Some communes applied for loans from the Agricultural Bank even when they had sufficient resources of their own. For instance, Hsu Hang Commune of Shanghai received a loan of ¥200,000 at a time when it had nearly a million yuan available in its reserve fund. The reason behind this is not irrational parsimony; the communes usually ask for bank assistance for those projects for which they do not possess the necessary technical know-how. The Agricultural Bank has trained agricultural scientists, architects, civil and mechanical engineers, hydrologists, geologists, etc. on its staff. Before a loan application is accepted by the bank, it has to be thoroughly examined by the technical staff. This technical scrutiny usually results in important changes being made in the project blueprints submitted by the commune. The communes can, and very often do, call upon the bank's technical personnel for help if the bank-supported projects run into technical difficulties.

Chapter IV

IMPORTANCE OF PRIVATE PLOTS

There is evidence that after the communization of the rural sector in China, all forms of private ownership disappeared. Private plots, allowed during the days of the cooperatives, were also transferred to the collectives. This period of total collectivization appears to have lasted for somewhat less than a year. In 1959 a small proportion of the collectivized areas was returned to private ownership. From Table 15 we can get some idea of the speed with which the local cadres implemented the decision of the central government to restore a part of the arable land to private ownership.

Table 15

Area Under Private Ownership in China, 1958-1964

Year	Arable Area	Area under private ownership (hectares)	Percentage of area under private ownership.
1958	5739 hectares	—	—
1959	5955 "	83	1.39
1960	5655 "	158	2.79
1961	5848 "	248	4.24
1962	6873 "	440	6.40
1963	7153 "	544	7.61
1964	7274 "	629	8.64

Note: These figures relate to Tsin Yah, Peng Pu, Hsu Hang and West Lake Communes. Only these communes provided detailed figures regarding the transfer of land from public to private ownership in the period 1958-1964.

By 1962 more than 6 per cent of the commune land fit for cultivation had been decollectivized. In 1964 the ten communes (see note, Table 16) taken together (we do not have the relevant figures for the Stonewell Commune of Kwangtung province), had 7.55 per cent of the cultivable land under private ownership. This was more than the declared objective of the government according to which not more than 5 per cent of the total cultivated land was to be given over to the peasants. Apparently the directives from the government eventually determined the floor rather than the ceiling for decollectivization.

Extent of Decollectivization

There was, however, considerable difference in the extent of decollectivization achieved in different communes (see Table 16 below). Peking's Evergreen Commune had only 4.96 per cent of the total cultivated land under private ownership. On the other hand, the Management Committee of Chekiang's West Lake Commune had, by July 1965, decollectivized 9.31 per cent of the entire cultivated area. The difference in the degree of decollectivization is

Table 16

Size and Incomes from Private Plots, 1964

No.	Commune	% of total area under private owner ship	Size of private plots	Net Income per hectare of private plot	Net income per communal hectare	Ratio of private and communal incomes per hectare
			(sq.met.)	(yuan)	(yuan)	
1.	Evergreen	4.96	171.6	12589.0	2494.3	5.05
2.	Red Star	6.42	655.4	8144.0	1291.7	6.30
3.	Kawkang	8.11	592.4	1542.4	603.7	2.55
4.	August First	7.99	971.4	2253.7	658.7	3.42
5.	Tsin Yah	8.57	1236.7	692.7	315.7	2.19
6.	Hsin Lung San	8.34	1113.5	345.7	319.7	1.08
7.	Peng Pu	8.14	209.6	7320.5	2503.4	2.93
8.	Hsu Hang	8.23	294.7	4109.5	1532.4	2.68
9.	West Lake	9.31	172.2	5967.7	3940.4	1.52
10.	Tung Chun	7.31	213.5	1906.9	1559.6	1.22

Note: We were not presented with any evidence of private ownership of land in the Leap Forward Commune of Inner Mongolia. However, in this commune, 4 per cent of the total animal population was owned privately by the herdsmen. The People's Suburban Commune, with 100 per cent of its income derived from fishing, had no private ownership of the means of production. Some land in Stonewell Commune had been decollectivized but we were not able to get the necessary data from the management of this commune. In the above table, as in most of the analysis that follows, we had to rely, therefore, on the statistics obtained from only ten communes.

considerably reduced by dropping the two Peking communes from this part
of the analysis. Both Evergreen and Red Star Communes are often visited by
foreigners and one can expect the conditions in them to be close to those
stated in official Chinese publications. Officially the government has not admitted
so far to having decollectivized more than 5 per cent of the total cultivated
land, a figure reflected very closely by the two Peking communes when considered together. We see from Table 16 that in the remaining communes
decollectivization had proceeded beyond the 5 per cent mark by August
1965. It seems fair to conclude from the evidence presented in the table
that, by 1965, slightly more than 8 per cent of the cultivated land had been
distributed to the peasants under the private plots scheme.

Productivity of Private and Communal Land

Table 16 gives an indication of the difference in the output derived from
privately and commonly owned land. In Evergreen Commune, peasants were
able to produce from the land they owned five times as much as they got out
of the communal land. In Hsin Lung San Commune, on the other hand, the
yields from the two types of lands were almost the same. In Table 16, income
figures for the commune land are the same as those given in Table 5 under the
item "net income", that is, gross income minus production costs, agricultural
tax, and contributions to the reserve and welfare funds. If we interpret net
output as gross income minus the production cost, the resulting income ratios
are somewhat lower. In this case (see Table 17) the ratios between the income
per hectare of privately and community owned lands are greater than one for
all but one commune.

Under a system in which the community owns the means of production,
private ownership and cultivation of land should be at a disadvantage. To
begin with, the community has first claim on the labor of able-bodied workers.
These workers can only attend to their private plots in their spare time. In
Chinese agriculture, labor is fully exploited; many production units take credit
for having worked their members for more than the required eight hours. By

38

Table 17

Ratio of Incomes from Private and Community Lands Derived under
a Different Set of Assumptions

No.	Commune	Net Income per hectare of priv. plots (yuan)	Net income per communal hectare (yuan)	Ratios of private and communal incomes per hectare
1.	Evergreen	12589.0	3293.3	3.82
2.	Red Star	8144.0	1975.5	4.12
3.	Kawkang	1542.4	768.7	1.99
4.	August First	2253.7	997.1	2.26
5.	Tsin Yah	692.7	398.4	1.74
6.	Hsin Lung San	345.7	399.1	0.87
7.	Peng Pu	7320.5	3412.5	2.15
8.	Hsu Hang	4109.5	2030.1	2.02
9.	West Lake	5967.7	4725.2	1.26
10.	Tung Chun	1906.9	1897.2	1.01

way of labor, private plots in China cannot, therefore, receive the best quality input. Also, the peasants in their private capacity do not have a ready access to new agricultural inputs like improved quality seeds, chemical fertilizer, insecticides etc. At least in the period before 1963, the peasants have had to rely totally on their own devices for cultivating their plots. Farmers cannot usually look for any advice from the agro-technicians working in their production units when it comes to the use of cultivable land in their private ownership. The farmers have to make do with the techniques they learn in their capacity as community workers. And, finally, the state does not provide an assured outlet for the produce of private plots. This produce has to be sold in the village fairs at whatever price the farmers can fetch. (We shall see below that, at times, this can be an advantage.)

Nevertheless, the private plots have helped Chinese agriculture to recover rapidly from the disaster of 1959-1961. Despite obstacles to their efficient utilization, these plots yield, on an average, more than twice as much as community owned land. We do not have to look very hard for the reasons. First, the government has classified the output of land into three categories. Into the first category fall all food grains, cotton and oil seeds, important industrial crops, some animal products; "resources for exports" belong to the second; and all the remaining agricultural products fall into the third category. First category output has to be handed over to the state trading corporations at predetermined prices. A certain fixed quantity of the second class of output has to be sold to the state corporations at a price mutually agreed upon between the government and the production units. Third category output can be sold in the open market (village fairs). Since the communes produce mainly first category products, prices for these products are unilaterally determined by the state. This gives a downward bias to the value of the commune output. The state quotas for the products belonging to the second class are met almost totally by the communes and this also results in the commune management and the peasants selling the same product (e.g. pork) at different prices. This gives a further downward bias to the value of the commune output. Second, the private plots specialize in the production of high-income products like pigs and vegetables while the bulk of the commune income comes from the production of grain. Third, ownership of land must also serve as a positive incentive.

Output per hectare of private plot varies from commune to commune. On the whole bigger plots have lower output per hectare. The rank coefficient of correlation between the size of private plots and their output is -0.62. This negative correlation may be explained in terms of diminishing returns which seem to set in fairly quickly in the case of private plots. Chinese peasants give first priority to pig breeding. However, a family is not allowed to keep more than three pigs at the same time. K.R. Walker has estimated in his study *(Planning in Chinese Agriculture,* Chicago: Aldine Publishing Company, 1965, p. 66) that it takes 134 and 20-27 square meters of land to provide feed for a pig in North and North-East China and Central and South-East China respectively. If this is a correct estimate then the entire privately owned land in Peking, about 40-46 per cent in Liaoning and Kirin provinces and 30-45 per cent in Shanghai and Chekiang provinces, is devoted to pig farming. Land that is left

40

over is used for growing vegetables. It is only in the communes of the northern parts of the country that the peasants produce food grains on the land they own. The yield of land used for pig breeding is between ¥ 1.2 - 1.5 per square meter, for vegetables between ¥ 0.7 -0.8 per square meter and for food grains only ¥ 0.3 per square meter. This means that as the size of the family plot increases the returns from it progessively decrease.

Increases from Private Plots

We can see from Table 18 that the income obtained from the private plots constitutes a significant proportion of the total family earnings. In 1964, private plots were the source of 30.2 per cent of the total peasant incomes of Peking's Red Star Commune. In Tung Chun Commune of Chekiang province, however, these plots yielded only 8.8 per cent of the total earnings of the peasant families. In the same year, for all the ten communes of Table 18 taken together, 19.3 per cent of the total family income was derived from privately owned plots. In these communes, however, the total area under private ownership in 1964 constituted only 7.6 per cent of the total land.

Table·18

Income from Private Plots as Percentage of Total Family Income

No.	Commune	Total income per family	Income received from the commune per family	Family income from private plot	Priv. Plot income as percentage of total income
		(yuan)	(yuan)	(yuan)	
1.	Evergreen	1037.0	821.0	216.0	20.8
2.	Red Star	1770.9	1236.4	534.5	30.2
3.	Kawkang	496.7	405.3	91.4	18.4
4.	August First	954.6	735.7	218.9	22.9
5.	Tsin Yah	501.3	415.6	85.7	17.1
6.	Hsin Lung San	482.4	390.9	81.5	16.9
7.	Peng Pu	745.5	592.0	153.5	20.6
8.	Hsu Hang	624.4	503.3	121.1	19.4
9.	West Lake	763.9	661.1	102.8	13.5
10.	Tung Chun	462.8	422.1	40.7	8.8

Chapter V

INCREASES IN INCOME AND PRODUCTIVITY

Significant increases in income over the period 1958-1964 were reported
by eleven of the thirteen communes we visited. (The Leap Forward Commune
of Inner Mongolia was formed in 1960 and the People's Suburban Commune
of Kiangsu was organized in 1961.) However, the data to show increases in
income as a result of communization were not supplied in the same form by
these communes. Some communes provided figures showing gross income at
different points of time, some gave statistics showing wages paid out to agricultural workers over the years, and some supplied data on the income received
by families in the years following communization. All these data have been
brought together in a consistent form in Table 20. However, lack of consistency
in the raw data may make it difficult to draw meaningful conclusions. Only
six communes were able to provide us with any idea of their gross incomes
in 1958. Three gave us figures showing income received per family in all the
seven years after communization and two gave us statistics for wages distributed
to the able-bodied workers. Net distributed income for 1958 for these five
communes have been calculated by multiplying the income per family in 1958
with the number of families in 1964 (or by multiplying the wages received per
agricultural worker by the number of able-bodied workers in 1964). Gross income figures were obtained by inflating the net distributed incomes by gross
income: distributed income ratios for the year 1964 (see Table 7). The fact
that the number of families as well as of able-bodied workers must have
increased in the period 1958-1964 would give an upward bias to the gross
income calculated for 1958 and a downward bias to percentage increases
between 1958 and 1964.

Gross income more than doubled in the period 1958-1964 in four communes. Two of these, Evergreen and Red Star, are in the Peking area and are
treated as model communes. The third, Tung Chun, though the poorest of the

Table 20

Gross Income of the Thirteen Communes in 1958 and 1964

No.	Commune	Gross Income (¥ million)		Percentage Increase
		1958	1964	
1.	Evergreen	5.320	13.300	150
2.	Red Star	12.000	27.000	125
3.	Leap Forward	—	0.250	—
4.	Kawkang	1.020	2.202	116
5.	August First+	1.510	3.900	93
6.	Tsin Yah+	1.250	2.250	80
7.	Hsin Lung San	5.290	6.600	24
8.	Peng Pu *	2.429	3.862	63
9.	Hsu Hang	3.100	4.250	39
10.	West Lake+	1.270	1.760	38
11.	Tung Chun*	0.625	1.320	111
12.	People's Suburban	—	1.100	—
13.	Stonewell	4.800	9.000	88

Note: +Gross Income figure for 1958 obtained from the figures for income received per family for the year 1958.

*Gross Income figure for 1958 obtained from the figures for income received per able-bodied worker in the year 1958.

thirteen communes visited by us, was cited as a "success story" by the officials of the Agriculture Department of Chekiang Province. The fourth, Kawkang Commune of Liaoning, had achieved the highest rate of investment in development schemes (investment per capita) in the period 1958-1964 in all of Northeast China.

Increase in Productivity

Rises in incomes were, of course, made possible by corresponding rises in land productivity. Table 21 summarizes some of the data presented to the delegation by some of the communes it visited. The yield per hectare of wheat-producing land increased from between 231 per cent to 442 per cent in the

Table 21

Output per Hectare of Land Producing Rice, Wheat, or Vegetables
in 1957 and 1964 (in kilograms)

Commune	Paddy Rice		Wheat		Vegetables	
	1957	1964	1957	1964	1957	1964
Red Star	1800	4700	800	3000	–	–
Kawkang	1300	5200	750	2950	–	–
August First	1425	5400	–	··	–	–
Tsin Yah	–	–	–	–	16000	23000
Hsin Lung San	–	–	–	–	9000	14500
Peng Pu	–	–	–	–	46500	90750
Hsu Hang	3870	7275	877	2910	–	–
West Lake	3475	7950	–	–	–	–
Tung Chun	2500	7530	–	–	–	–
Stonewell	5310	8430	–	–	–	–

Note: In Tsin Yah Commune, the yield of coarse grains went up from 1139 kilograms per
hectare in 1957 to 1359 kilograms in 1964. In Hsin Lung San Commune, per hectare yield of
coarse grain increased from 1400 kilograms to 1550 kilograms. In Hsu Hang Commune, yield
of cotton per hectare increased from 285 kilograms in 1957 to 607 kilograms in 1964.

period 1957-1964 in the three communes of Red Star, Kawkang, and Hsu
Hang. The yield of rice registered a rise of between 59 per cent and 300 per cent.
However, relatively modest yield increases were obtained in the case of land
devoted to vegetable production; here the output per hectare rose by between
41 per cent and 95 per cent. Investment in water conservancy, land improvement, and irrigation projects; greater use of chemical fertilizers and insecticides;
more intensive use of land; improvement in farming techniques; and greater
mechanization were cited as reasons for these increases in productivity (see
in Appendix the sub-heading "Reasons for Success" under all the communes).
We deal in some detail with a few of these factors:

Increased use of chemical fertilizer

"Greater and more scientific use of chemical fertilizer" was given a very
prominent place in The Eight-Point Charter which guided communization in

46

China (see Chapter I). However, the two really big spurts in the use of chemical fertilizer came before communization; in 1954-1955, the use of chemical fertilizer went up by 57.5 per cent and in 1957-1958 by 40.2 per cent. The immediate result of communization appears to have been a reversal of this trend. In 1959, only 9.9 per cent more chemical fertilizer was used as compared with 1958 (See Table 3). Only two communes provided us with statistics for yearly use of fertilizer since 1958. These figures (Table 22), however, tell a different story. According to them, communization led to an immediate increase in the use of chemical fertilizer.

Table 22

Rise in the Use of Chemical Fertilizer in Evergreen and Hsu Hang Communes
1958-1964

Year	Amount of Fertilizer Used (tons)*	Rate of Increase (per cent)
1958	421	—
1959	764	81.5
1960	957	25.2
1961	1040	8.7
1962	1090	4.6
1963	1200	10.1
1964	1660	38.3

Note: *The amounts are for Evergreen and Hsu Hang Communes taken together.

Table 23 provides data showing the use of fertilizer per cultivated hectare in eleven of the thirteen communes visited by the delegation. The grass-lands commune of Inner Mongolia and the fishing commune of Kiangsu did not, of course, use any chemical fertilizer. We noticed above that the land producing vegetables had shown only moderate increases in yields as compared to the lands used for growing wheat and rice. Of the three communes which provided statistics on vegetable output per hectare, two (Tsin Yah and Hsin Lung San) used very small amounts of fertilizer. From this we may conclude

Table 23

Use of Chemical Fertilizer per Hectare of Cultivated Land

No.	Commune	Amount Used (kilograms)
1.	Evergreen	427.8
2.	Red Star	373.3
3.	Kawkang	212.7
4.	August First	235.2
5.	Tsin Yah	34.7
6.	Hsin Lung San	14.8
7.	Peng Pu	451.7
8.	Hsu Hang	276.4
9.	West Lake	1000.0
10.	Tung Chun	398.0
11.	Stonewell	225.0

that increases in vegetable yields were deliberately kept down by not allowing the communes producing mostly vegetables to go in for heavy fertilization. However, this conclusion goes against the assertion of most of the offficials belonging to the agricultural departments. According to them non-grain producing land had been given priority in the use of chemical fertilizer (see Appendix: VII,7).

Increased Mechanization

We do not have the data showing the extent of mechanization before com- munization. Table 1 above indicates a steady increase in mechanization in the post-1958 period. The rate of increase reached its peak in the period 1960-1961. By 1964, Chinese agriculture employed machinery producing 7 million horse- power; of this, 4 million horsepower was produced by pumping equipment. Table 24 provides an indication of the use of mechanical equipment in the communes visited by the delegation.

Table 24

Use of Mechanical Equipment in the Communes, 1964

No.	Commune	Horsepower per Cultivated Hectare
1.	Evergreen	0.15
2.	Red Star	0.29
3.	Kawkang	0.45
4.	August First	0.16
5.	Tsin Yah	0.05
6.	Hsin Lung San	0.14
7.	Peng Pu	2.39
8.	Hsu Hang	0.99
9.	West Lake	0.06
10.	Tung Chun	0.90
11.	Stonewell	11.00

Note: All communes did not provide data indicating the total power of the mechanical equipment in use. In their case, the total horsepower of the equipment was calculated by assuming 10 horsepower for each mobile water pump, 20 horsepower for each tractor, and 50 horsepower for each pumping station in use. Details of the equipment in use can be found in the Appendix under the sub-heading "Capital Construction".

Agricultural Research

In China, research in agriculture is the responsibility of a very elaborate, multi-tiered organization. At the top of the organization is the Academy of Agricultural Sciences located at Peking. It was founded in 1957 under the Chinese Ministry of Agriculture. The academy started with 10 departments and 400 trained technicians; in 1965 it had 27 departments and 21,000 technicians. Out of its 21,000 technical experts, 15,000 are posted in various parts of the country.

The research organization closely follows the province-county-commune-production team structure. All provinces have their agricultural research institutes. These are controlled jointly by the provincial departments of agriculture and the Peking Academy. Close affiliation with the academy gives a meaningful direction to the research efforts of these institutes. Suggestions for experimental research are often received from Peking and conducted under the supervision of the academy technicians. Such a vast feed-in mechanism is important for the academy because it can develop methods that become economical because of their wide applicability in tackling outstanding problems.

All the counties have agricultural research sections. These are actually located within the communes but are managed by the technical staff of the county office of agriculture. These experimental stations provide research facilities for Peking Academy, provincial institutes, and county technical experts. They are also used by the agricultural colleges.

APPENDIX

The Communes

Note:- The data provided in this Appendix, one section for each commune
visited by the delegation, refer to 1965. Each section has seventeen
sub-heads; each sub-head refers to a different aspect of communal
life or of the developmental history of the commune. In some sections,
only the sub-headings appear, without any data pertaining to them.
This is so because not all the commune directors provided us with the
same kind of information.

I

EVERGREEN

1. *Date of Formation:* The commune was established in August 1958 by
merging eleven cooperatives. It is also called China-Bulgaria Friendship
Commune.

2. *Location:* 23 km. from Peking.

3. *Population:* 8,100 peasant families live in 116 villages. Out of a total
population of 36,000 the Commune Management Committee lists 14,000
as able-bodied workers.

4. *Land:* The commune has 3120 hectares of farm land. 2805 hectares, or
nearly 90 per cent are cultivated. Only 58 per cent of the total area was
being cultivated in 1958. The land is virtually flat which makes it easier
to irrigate. 533 hectares have been provided with irrigation water from
electric tubewells.

5. *Crops:* 88 of the 125 production teams grow only vegetables. Vegetables
are produced all the year round. In 1964, the commune sold 115,000 tons
of vegetables for consumption in Peking. This is one and a half times
more than in the days of the cooperatives. The commune also sold 2,430
tons of fruit which is sixty-four times the amount of fruit marketed in
1958. 37 production teams also produce wheat, sorghum, and millet.

6. *Sources of Income:* 80 per cent of the crop income is derived from the sale of vegetables to the Vegetable State Trading Corporation. The second major source of income is a noodle factory which employs 100 able-bodied workers. The main source of income for the Commune Management Committee is an Agricultural Implement Repair Workshop which employs 110 workers. The workshop has ten new and old lathes, four of which are operated by girls. The commune also owns and operates 35 trucks, 19 tractors, 40 hand tillers and a threshing machine. When it was established, the commune had only 4 trucks but no tractors. The gross income of the commune has increased from ¥7 million in 1958 to ¥13.3 million in 1964.

7. *Capital Construction:* Over the period 1958-1964, the commune and its production teams have contributed ¥5.74 million to the Commune Reserve Fund. Out of this, ¥3.89 million has been spent on land improvement, provision of irrigation water, purchase of equipment for the workshop, and purchase of agricultural implements. The biggest work undertaken by the commune so far was the digging of a canal for which 2,000 workers were mobilized over a period of 100 days. Contributions from the reserve fund were also used for digging 412 wells. All of these have now been provided with electric pumps. The commune has received no assistance from the state.

8. *Bureaucracy:* Mr. Kao is the director of the commune. He belongs to the area that now constitutes the commune and once owned one hectare of vegetable-producing land. He is 47 years old and has been a government cadre for 11 years and commune director for 4 years. He was appointed a member of the management committee in 1958 after he had received 6 weeks of intensive training in Peking for commune management. He receives ¥65 per month and also spends 60 days working in the fields for which he does not receive any extra remuneration. His wife manages the private plot which yields an income of ¥30 per month. There are in all 15 cadres working in the commune.

9. *Training in Agriculture:* The commune operates an agricultural experimental station with the help of the students from Peking's Agricultural Academy. There is a special department of agricultural research working under one of the members of the management committee. The department transmits information obtained from the experimental station to selected farmers and keeps a record of the activities of these farmers.

10. *Health Facilities:* The commune has one 30-bed hospital and 9 clinics. Thirty-two trained doctors work in the commune area.

11. *Educational Facilities:* In 1958 the commune had ten primary schools with a total enrollment of 3,800. Since then seven new primary schools have been opened and the enrollment has jumped to 6,000. The commune is also operating four middle schools with a total enrollment of 2,500. The commune's department of agricultural research also runs an agro-technical school which has 50 students. Five primary schools, two middle schools and the agro-technical school have new buildings, the rest are housed either in old buildings or in community halls put up hurriedly in 1958. The commune has purchased ¥40,000 worth of equipment for the agro-technical school. The school was described to be self-supporting in the sense that the income from the seven-hectare farm attached to it is used for paying salaries to the six teachers. All the teachers come from within the commune.

12. *Recreational Facilities:*

13. *Marketing:* The State Supply and Marketing Corporation has set up 40 retail shops within the commune. The shops are managed by the brigade management committees and are located in the bigger villages. The shops stock and sell goods like cycles, watches, radio sets, china ware, and groceries. Ultimately the commune management hopes to locate a shop in each of the 116 villages. 60 per cent of the families now own radio sets and 70 per cent have bicycles. We visited a shop located in the headquarters of the Nan Pin Chan Production Brigade. Mr. Han, the shop-keeper, is a full-time employee of the brigade. He runs his business in a thatch-roofed room with mud-plastered walls and floor. The shop is well

stocked. It was set up in 1960 and in the past five years it has sold 126 bicycles, 172 wrist watches, 112 radio sets and 52 sewing machines to the members of the production brigade which number 2,400.

14. *Banking:* Members of the commune deposit their savings with the Credit Cooperative Society. 4,200 families have so far opened savings accounts in the society's five offices. Their total deposits have exceeded the ¥1 million mark.

15. *Industry:* The commune operates thirteen industrial units with a total employment of 500. The biggest is a noodle factory. The commune also runs two ceramic factories and one agricultural implement manufacturing shop. A creamery operated by the commune supplies butter, cheese, and other milk products to the brigade retail shops.

16. *Animal husbandry:* There are 2,000 collectively owned animals. These include 100 dairy cows, 115 horses, 127 donkeys, and 376 pigs. 17,000 pigs are owned privately by the farmers.

17. *Reasons for Success:* The director of the commune ascribed the doubling of the gross income in 6 years to the following factors: 40 per cent to improved agricultural practices, 25 per cent to land improvement and irrigation, 25 per cent to better management and 10 per cent to other causes.

II
RED STAR

1. *Date of Formation:* The commune was formed in September, 1958, with the merger of seven Advanced Agricultural Producers' Cooperatives. The commune is also called the China-Korea Friendship Commune.

2. *Location:* 33 km. from Peking.

3. *Population:* The commune has 11,000 peasant families with a total population of 55,000 living in 96 villages. There are 24,000 able-bodied workers.

4. *Land:* Out of 13,700 hectares of land owned by the commune, 11,251 hectares are cultivated or used for dairy farming and stock breeding. Before 1958, water logging was a major problem. There were no adequate drainage facilities and good land was being rapidly lost to cultivation. Now the commune has recovered all the lost land; it has more than 9,000 hectares under irrigation.

5. *Crops:* Wheat is the major crop, though not the main source of income for the commune. Rice is also grown. Both crops have registered a high increase in productivity since 1958. Wheat yield has gone up from 800 kg/hectare to 3,000 kg per hectare. Paddy yield has increased from 1800 kg to 4,700 kg. In 1964, 800,000 tons of fruit, 140,000 tons of vegetables, 15,000 kg of fish and 11,000 tons of milk were sold in the Peking market. Of the 157 production teams, 40 specialize in the production of dairy products and the famous Peking duck (Beijing ya).

6. *Sources of Income:* The commune has a gross income of ¥27.00 million. Of this, agriculture yielded ¥12.00 million, industry ¥8.0 million and poultry ¥7.0 million. The 40 specialized production teams are directly controlled by the Commune Management Committee. The committee also runs a packing-paper manufacturing plant which uses rice straw as raw material.

7. *Capital Construction:* The commune and other production units have contributed ¥15.0 million to the reserve fund in the period 1958-1964. Out of this, ¥10.7 million have been spent on soil improvement, irrigation,

and drainage projects. Three big canals with a total length of 60 km. have been excavated by the commune. Apart from harvesting, all other agricultural work has been mechanized. The commune now owns 25 trucks and 64 tractors. In 1958 the commune had only 5 trucks and 16 tractors. In 1958 there were only 50 wells; now there are 200 of them, all equipped with electric pumps. The commune has also purchased 11 harvester-combines, a butter-making machine, and equipment for producing powdered milk. No assistance has been received from the state capital lending agencies.

8. *Bureaucracy:* Mr. Yuan was elected the director in 1958. He is 53 years old and was a farm worker before land reform in 1950. Mr. Yuan's commune secretariat is made up of 11 departments, each under a government cadre.

9. *Training in Agriculture:* The commune has finished plans for setting up an agro-technical school in October. The commune is already operating a seed-breeding station and a veterinary research center. An artificial insemination unit of the center serves all the animal population of the commune. No natural service is provided at all to horses and cattle.

10. *Health Facilities:* The commune has no hospital. All cases requiring hospitalization are taken to Peking. There are nine fairly well equipped clinics, each serving a production brigade. In all 40 doctors work in these clinics.

11. *Educational Facilities:* The commune has fifteen primary and six secondary schools with a total enrollment of 11,000. The agro-technical school to be set up in October will have 50 students.

12. *Recreational Facilities:* All the nine production brigades have recreational centers. Six of these are equipped with film projectors. All the centers have TV sets.

13. *Marketing:* The State Supply and Marketing Corporation has set up 63 retail shops in the commune area.

14. *Banking:* 7,200 families have accounts in the branches of the Credit Cooperation Society. The total deposits in these accounts is more than

¥2.2 million. The society has been assisting the people in building their own houses. A new house with one bedroom, one living room, and a bathroom costs ¥2,000.

15. *Industry:* The commune operates a number of industrial enterprises. The packing-paper plant employs 520 workers and yields a total income of ¥250,000. A mechanized brick kiln employs 480 workers and yields an income of ¥100,000.

16. *Animal Husbandry:* The commune has a large animal population. There are 20 pig breeding farms with 30,000 pigs. The commune's nine duck farms produce 40,000 birds per annum. Forced feeding of ducks has reduced the period of maturation to 60 days. The average yield of milk is 16 kg per head of cattle per day.

17. *Reasons for Success:* The director gave the following reasons for the increase in the income of the commune: a) improved irrigational facilities, b) increased use of farmyard manure; 30,000 kg/hectare of natural manure was being used, c) greater use of chemical fertilizer; 400 kg of chemical fertilizer were being used per hectare, d) agro-technical advances had been made in several directions. For instance, the commune was using ammonia solution instead of ammonium sulphate for soil fertilization.

III
LEAP FORWARD

1. *Date of Formation:* The commune was formed in 1960. It differs from other communes we visited in the sense that it has no production brigades. The commune is divided into 48 production teams.

2. *Location:* 23 km. from Selinhot, administrative headquarters of Silingol League, one of the seven leagues into which the Autonomous Region of Inner Mongolia is divided. The leagues are further divided into banners; Leap Forward Commune is located in Akhul Banner. Silingol League has 122 communes in all.

3. *Population:* The commune is made up of 252 families which have a total population of 776. There are 350 able-bodied workers of whom 159 are men and 191 women. At the time of the formation of the commune, there were only 133 families with a population of 428. A growth in population of more than 81 per cent in five years is partly due to natural increase and partly due to reorganization of nomadic tribes undertaken after the communization of the area. Efforts are being made all over Inner Mongolia to increase the population; in this commune 192 children were born in just over five years.

4. *Land:* The commune covers an area of 1,660 sq. km. of grass land. The grass land is divided into four regions and only one of them is occupied at one time by herdsmen. Herdsmen spend four to six months in one region.

5. *Crops:*

6. *Sources of Income:* Animals and animal products are the main sources of income. The commune sells live animals, wool, milk, sheep skins, fermented horse milk, cottage cheese, and butter to the State Trading Corporations. The commune also earns from 10 to 12 per cent of its total income by the sale of camel seats, leather belts, embroided cushions, etc. to the state. Most of the handicrafts are produced by workers but raw material is provided by the Commune Management Committee.

7. *Capital Construction:* Over the last five years, the commune has constructed 31 barns, each of which can accommodate 2,000 to 3,000 animals. In the same period, 18 mowers and 14 hay collectors have also been purchased. The commune also owns 11 rubber-tired carts, and 14 iron-wheeled carts. The commune has saved less than 70,000 yuan in its reserve fund since its formation. The main reason for this low accumulation is that it has been distributing between 70 to 75 per cent of its gross income among its members. The state has given ¥50,000 as a grant to the commune.

8. *Bureaucracy:* Mr. Pai is the director. Besides him, there is only one other government cadre in the commune. Both of them joined the government after the Communists took over Inner Mongolia.

9. *Training in Agriculture:*

10. *Health Facilities:* No doctors served in this area before the formation of the commune. Now a mobile clinic has been set up which employs five doctors and twelve nurses.

11. *Educational Facilities:* In 1950 all the herdsmen were totally illiterate. Now 196 can read and write. Twenty families have daughters receiving their education in Selinhot. Six young men are studying in the Inner Mongolia Animal Husbandry and Agriculture College at Huhehot. A building for a primary school is being erected at Akhul Banner with the assistance of the government.

12. *Recreational Facilities:* All the banner headquarters have reading rooms which are supplied with national and Mongolian literature. The commune takes part in the annual dance and music show at Selinhot. One of its members has been performing as a professional in the Inner Mongolian Dance Troupe which has toured all parts of China. The state encourages horse-racing, tent-pegging, marksmanship, and herd-management by organizing competitions in all the leagues of the region.

13. *Marketing:* The commune members buy their food grains and other necessities from the commune-operated cooperative store. The State Supply and Marketing Corporation was doing no business in Inner Mongolia;

all retail businesses were being run by the communes themselves. On an average, the meat consumption of a commune member amounts to six animals per year. Some of this comes from the stocks privately owned by the herdsmen and the rest is bought from the commune cooperative store. The store also sells flannel-lined tents to the herdsmen. This kind of tent has been especially developed by the Inner Mongolian Research Institute at Huhehot and serves adequately to protect the herdsmen against the rigors of the Mongolian climate. All 252 families now own these tents. All of them have transistorized radio sets and alarm clocks; 73 possess sewing machines.

14. *Banking:*

15. *Industry:* The commune proposes to set up a small dairy plant at Akhul. An application for a grant-in-aid from the government has been made by the commune to cover part of the capital cost of the plant. The application has been pending for consideration at Huhehot for more than a year. (On returning to Huhehot, we made inquiries about this. We were told by the Regional Director of Animal Husbandry that such an application had, in fact, been received but was not likely to be agreed to since the implementation of the dairy plant project would place a heavy financial burden on the commune. To meet the cost of the project, the commune would have to cut down the proportion of income distributed among the farmers from 70 per cent to 50 per cent of the total. This was against the policy of the government because it wanted the herdsmen to enjoy a high standard of living. Besides, in his view, small, scattered dairy plants of the type Leap Forward Commune wanted to establish would prove uneconomical over the long run. The state was, instead, endeavoring to set up food-processing industries in all the seven league headquarters.)

16. *Animal Husbandry:* At the time of its formation the commune had only 37,000 animals. Their number had now increased to 72,000. Four per cent of the animals were owned by the people.

IV
KAWKANG

1. *Date of Formation:* The commune was formed in September, 1958.

2. *Location:* The commune is located between the twin industrial cities of Shenyang and Fuchang. Its headquarters is situated about 35 km. from Shenyang. A motorable road connects the commune with Fuchang and Shenyang.

3. *Population:* The commune's 2,988 peasant families have a total population of 15,000. There are 24 villages in the commune. There are 4,000 able-bodied workers.

4. *Land:* Out of 5,000 hectares of semi-mountainous country, 2,183 hectares are under cultivation. Only 1,473 hectares were being cultivated before 1958. A number of factors are responsible for this increase in area under cultivation. The peasants have been taught new ways of plugging gullies and terracing land for cultivation. In this way water which used to run off is now being held back for irrigation.

5. *Crops:* Before 1958 the area which now makes up the commune country produced upland rice, maize, millet, and sorghum. After the formation of the commune, four-fifths of the cultivated area was turned over to vegetable farming. This switch from grains to vegetables was described by the commune administration as part of the program of rationalization launched after communization. In 1957 the area which is now under the management of the commune produced 1.16 million kg of green vegetables. In 1964 the commune produced 10.0 million kg of which 9.5 million kg was marketed in Shenyang and Fuchang.

6. *Sources of Income:* Vegetable production provides the commune with its main source of income. Animal husbandry is the second important source of income. In fact, there has been a big advance in this field since 1958. The commune directly controls two dairy farms with 120 cattle. It also owns 200 sheep and 600 pigs. The sheep and pig farms

provide all the commune's production units with manure. This is sold
to the production teams by the Commune Management Committee.
The third major source of income for the commune is a stone and gravel
quarry which feeds a cement factory located in Shenyang. The Commune
Management Committee has bought two dump trucks to carry stone
and gravel to the factory. The commune also sells medicinal herbs to
the State Trading Corporation.

7. *Capital Construction:* The total investment in various agricultural improve-
    ment schemes since 1958 amounts to ¥1.5 million. The commune has
    not received any assistance from the state lending organizations. In the
    period 1958-1964 the commune constructed three big pumping stations
    for lifting water from the river. Each station has a capacity of 400 horse-
    power. Forty-eight electric wells were also constructed in the same period.
    Pumping stations and wells have brought more than 700 hectares of land
    under cultivation.

    The commune has also installed electric lines to bring power from Shenyang
    to its villages. All the houses in the commune have been electrified, all
    water pumps are power operated and all milling and threshing is done
    with the help of power driven machines. The Commune Management Com-
    mittee now proposes to provide electric power to its hothouse.

8. *Bureaucracy:* Mr. Ching, 40 years old and a cadre, is the commune director.
    Eleven other cadres have also been appointed by the county to work in
    the commune. The Commune Secretariat is made up of ten departments
    which are responsible for general administration; finance and accounting; civil
    affairs; education and culture; public health; people's militia; agricultural
    production; women's activities; youth clubs; and workshop management.
    All the department heads are cadres who are also the members of the
    thirteen member Commune Management Committee. Two deputy
    directors help the director to look after the day-to-day management of
    the commune affairs.

9. *Training in Agriculture:* The Shenyang Agricultural College has been allotted three demonstration plots within the commune. These are part of the agricultural research set-up in the commune which includes an agro-technical college run by the county council, two agro-middle schools set up and run by the Commune Management Committee and eleven primary agricultural research stations run jointly by the commune and production teams. These institutions have produced 211 agro-technicians in the past six years. Of these 18 have gone on for higher studies in Shenyang and Fuchang. The commune has a special construction squad; all its 29 members have been trained in these institutions. The squad is responsible for planning, executing, and supervising development schemes within the commune. The Shenyang Agricultural College is now planning to set up a special institution which will impart to the members of the Kawkang Commune as well as those in the neighborhood, the technique of reclaiming water-eroded land. Outside participants would come and stay in the commune for three months and earn wages like the members of the commune.

10. *Health:* The commune is operating an 18-bed hospital in the headquarters village. All the 11 production brigades have been provided with adequately staffed clinics.

11. *Education:* Two secondary schools and nine primary schools are functioning within the commune. One secondary school is run by the state and the other is managed by the commune. The total enrollment in all the schools is over 4,000.

12. *Recreational Facilities:* Cultural troupes from Shenyang and Fuchang pay regular visits to the commune and perform in a community hall constructed by the Commune Management Committee in 1962. All the production brigades have their own basketball teams. The Commune Management Committee holds sport rallies during the slack agricultural seasons to which all the production teams send participants.

13. *Marketing:* The State Supply and Marketing Corporation has set up retail consumer stores in all the 59 production teams. From these stores, 754

wrist watches, 1,000 alarm clocks, 1008 radio sets, and 414 bicycles had been purchased as of 1964.

14. *Banking:* The commune members deposit their savings with the Credit Cooperative Society. Total deposits in 1964 amounted to ¥272,000. The Cooperative Society has advanced ¥110,000 to the commune members for house building purposes. Between 1958 and 1964, 857 private houses had been constructed.

15. *Industry:* Various production units have their own grain-milling machines. There are 30 such machines in the commune. The Commune Management Committee is now seeking state assistance for a vegetable drying and packing plant. The plant is expected to cost ¥200,000. Forty per cent of the total cost would be met by the commune from its own resources.

16. *Animal Husbandry:* See also Sources of Income. The commune members keep more than 7,200 pigs in their private plots.

17. *Reasons for Success:* The commune has not done as well as some other communes in this region. The director cited the following "problems and difficulties," a) mechanization has not proceeded very far, b) not enough fertilizer is being used, c) the commune's income is not sufficient to allow the execution of all the development schemes that have been approved by the county administration.

V
AUGUST FIRST

1. *Date of Formation:* The commune was formed in October, 1958. It was reduced in size in 1961 when a program of reorganization was undertaken in Liaoning province.

2. *Location:* It is situated about 30 km. from Shenyang, the capital city of Liaoning province. It derives its name from the People's Liberation Army Day which falls on August 1. The army helped the commune complete a 78 km. long canal in 18 days, thus making the water of the Hun River available for irrigation.

3. *Population:* The commune's 2,800 families have a total population of 13,390 living in 72 villages. There are 4,400 able-bodied workers, of whom 2,300 are women and 2,100 men.

4. *Land:* Total cultivated land is 3,401 hectares out of which 2,800 hectares are sown to paddy rice. Waterlogging was a great problem before 1958 but since then 90 per cent of the land has been rehabilitated. The August First Canal has brought nearly 1,000 hectares under irrigation.

5. *Crops:* Rice is the main crop. Vegetables and fruits are also grown. For this purpose the commune has provided 12,000 sq. meters of hothouse space.

6. *Sources of Income:* Paddy cultivation is the main source of income. The commune also runs a number of small industrial enterprises. These include five brick kilns, eight units for producing soyabean curd and noodles, six blacksmith and carpentry shops, three grain-milling shops, and 250 mat-weaving centers. All but the last are owned and operated by the Commune Management Committee. The mat-weaving shops are under the management of the production teams. In 1958 the commune had set up a paper mill; it was dismantled in 1961. In the period 1958-1960, 12 of the 14 brigades also operated their backyard furnaces.

7. *Capital Construction:* Since 1958, the commune has undertaken extensive water-conservancy, irrigation, and drainage projects. An amount of ¥1.5 million has been spent on these projects. This has been drawn from the reserve fund which has received total deposits of ¥3.1 million. No help has been solicited from the government; an offer of an interest-free loan of ¥500,000 made by the Agricultural Bank of China was turned down. The commune has also purchased 18 tractors, 5 trucks, and machinery for a pumping station. Electric cables for distributing power to the pumping station and rice-milling shops and for use in private houses have also been installed by the commune. All private dwellings now have electric connections. The commune has also undertaken an extensive afforestation program. Four hundred thousand trees have been planted along road sides and on canal banks. A fish culture program has also been successfully completed and for this purpose six special ponds have been provided. The hothouse will be provided with electric power this year.

8. *Bureaucracy:* Mr. Wang has been the director of the commune for the last five years. He has had five years of schooling. Mr. Fang is the deputy director and has been assigned only very recently to the commune. He has been to an agro-technical school. The Commune Secretariat has six offices responsible for general administration, agriculture, civil affairs, culture and education, finance and accounts, and civil militia. Every office has a government cadre in charge. There are in all 13 cadres working in the commune. The Commune Management Committee has 30 members, of whom 7 are cadres.

9. *Training in Agriculture:* The commune has been provided with an agro-technical dissemination center. The center has been equipped and staffed by the county. It has eight technicians. Three technicians hold university degrees and five have graduated from the local agro-technical school. The dissemination center works as the research arm of the agro-technical school. The school is run on a part-work, part-study pattern. This means that the students have to spend at least four hours every day working with

the peasants in the field. In this way they are able to earn their way through school and the peasants benefit by learning new and scientific farming techniques from these young workers.

10. *Health Facilities:* An old community dining room has been converted into an eighteen-bed ward for the commune hospital. The old kitchen is used by the four doctors working here as their surgery. The pantry has been converted into an examination room for out-patients. The job of reconstruction has been done by the commune under the advice of a health technician whose services were loaned by the county. The hospital is adequately equipped. The commune has no plans to construct a new building. All the production brigades have small clinics located in their headquarter villages.

11. *Educational Facilities:* Two secondary schools and nine primary schools are functioning within the commune. Of the two secondary schools, one is run by the state and the other by the commune Department of Culture and Education. The commune has achieved a literacy rate of 85 per cent.

12. *Recreational Facilities:* The commune has its own opera team. Three years ago they acted as the chorus for the troupe that performed "East is Red" in Shenyang. The commune's basketball team has also successfully participated in county and provincial games.

13. *Marketing:* The State Supply and Marketing Corporation has set up retail stores in all the 59 production teams. These stores can meet all the day-to-day requirements of the peasants and their families. Since 1958, the commune members have purchased 754 wrist watches, 1,000 alarm clocks, 1,008 radio sets, and 414 bicycles from these stores. The Marketing Corporation works as a cooperative. It has a working capital of ¥200,000. The cost of a cooperative share is three yuan. Profits are distributed according to the following formula: 50 per cent on the basis of the shares purchased and 50 per cent on the basis of the purchases made from the retail stores.

14. *Banking:* The commune members deposit their savings with the Credit Cooperative Society. The society advances loans to the people for building

houses. Eight hundred and fifty-seven new houses have been constructed in the last five years.

15. *Industry:* See Sources of Income.

16. *Animal Husbandry:*

17. *Reasons for Success:* The per capita income has more than doubled in the last six years. We were told of a number of success stories. For instance, Mr. Teche, a beggar before 1958, is now a full time able-bodied worker. He has a family of five; he owns a house, a radio, and a wrist watch. His wife has recently acquired a sewing machine. Two of his sons are studying in a college at Shenyang and a daughter is at present enrolled in the commune secondary school. Mr. Wang gave the following reasons for this rapid increase in per capita income: a) organized communal labor which was able to solve the waterlogging problem, b) dissemination of improved agricultural practices, c) rapid rise in literacy, d) cooperation of the county administration.

VI
TSIN YAH

1. *Date of Formation:* The commune was formed in November, 1958, with
    the amalgamation of 22 Advanced Agricultural Producers' Cooperatives.
    It then had 11 production brigades and 148 production teams. It was
    reorganized in 1961 when its size was considerably reduced. It now has
    7 production brigades and 87 production teams.

2. *Location:* The commune is located 15 km. from Changchun, the capital
    city of Kirin province.

3. *Population:* The commune's 3,000 families have a total population of
    15,252 of whom 4,800 are listed as able-bodied workers. There are 1,900
    full time women workers in the labor force.

4. *Land:* Of the commune's total estimated 6,200 hectares, 4,329 are
    cultivated. 546 hectares are under irrigation.

5. *Crops:* Food grains are grown in the plains which form the western part
    of the commune. In the eastern part, which is mostly hilly, vegetables
    are cultivated all the year round. One production brigade, administered
    directly by the Commune Management Committee, grows vegetables in
    hothouses. Another production brigade supplies pork to the commune
    members and is also administered directly by the Commune Management
    Committee.

6. *Sources of Income:* The bulk of the commune's income comes from the
    sale of wheat, sorghum, millet, and upland rice to the State Trading Corpora-
    tion. However, after the formation of the commune, its sources of income
    have been considerably diversified. Before 1958 there was little vegetable
    and hardly any fruit cultivation. Now the commune sells 12.5 million kg.
    of vegetables to the state every year out of which 75,000 kg. are grown
    in hothouses. In 1964 the state purchased 25,000 kg. of high quality
    fruit from the commune. In the same year 1,100 pigs, 2906 table birds,
    8,160 kg. of eggs and 22 tons of milk were also sold to the state. Nearly

50,000 yuan were earned by the sale of medicinal herbs to the State Pharmaceutical Corporation. Side occupations (that is other than grain and vegetable production) yield a total income of ¥ 3 million every year.

7. *Capital Construction:* Contributions made to the reserve fund in the period 1958-1964 total ¥1.3 million. All of this has been spent on various land improvement schemes. Two reservoirs (total storage capacity of 1 m. cubic meters) and 90 electric wells have brought 546 hectares of land under irrigation. The water logging problem has been almost totally solved with the help of a drainage network made up of 62 ditches and 47 km. of channels. This has helped to drain 1,100 hectares of land. Six out of the commune's seven brigades and 58 out of 59 production teams have electrified their principal villages. Seventy per cent of the dwelling houses have power connections. Reserve fund accumulations have also been used for purchasing three trucks. The commune has no tractors but proposes to acquire three in the course of the next year, provided the loan application made for this purpose is accepted by the Agricultural Bank. Before 1961, the commune was able to finance its development plans from its own resources. This has not been possible after the reorganization of 1961 because the richer areas were separated out to form a new commune. This was done to insure better state help for the poorer areas. Since 1961, this commune has received ¥1.5 million from the state as a loan carrying a 4 per cent per month rate of interest. The Chang-Chun Suburban Areas People's Council, which controls all the communes near the capital city, adjudicated the dispute which developed between the two communes carved out of Tsin Yah of pre-1961 days. It has now been settled that the Tsin Yah will pay ¥350,000 to the Second People's Suburban Commune over a ten-year period to compensate the latter for expenditures incurred in the territory of the former in the period 1958-1961. To make it possible for Tsin Yah to meet this obligation, the Agricultural Bank has agreed to advance a special loan of ¥300,000 payable over a twenty-year period at a 33 per cent per month rate of interest.

8. *Bureaucracy:* Mr. Wang is the director of the commune. The Commune Management Committee has 17 members, 7 of whom are cadres. The committee meets four times a year. The commune is controlled by Changchun Suburban Area People's Council. The council is a large body of men to which Tsin Yah alone sends 20 members.

9. *Training in Agriculture:* There are three centers working in the commune to impart instruction in new agricultural techniques to the members. The Agro-Technical Dissemination Center uses an experimental farm for teaching purposes. It employs two graduates as full-time workers. The Animal Husbandry and Veterinary Station provides training to the members of the special pig-breeding production brigades and other peasants directly engaged in stock breeding. The small tractor operator training station has been set up in anticipation of the arrival of three tractors now being demanded by the commune.

10. *Health Facilities:* A 15-bed hospital run by the commune and clinics in all the seven production brigades provide health facilities to the members.

11. *Educational Facilities:* The state runs one secondary, two middle and six primary schools in the commune territory. The commune runs one agriculture middle school and 30 primary schools. The total enrollment in all these institutions is 4,000. The agriculture middle school has 70 students.

12. *Recreational Facilities:* The commune has set up a broadcasting station in the headquarters village. This station feeds receiving and amplification stations in all the production brigade headquarters. Every production team has a study room well supplied with newspapers, magazines, and books. A small printing shop run by the commune produces wall posters to educate the members in the policies of the Communist Party.

13. *Marketing:* Retail shops run by the State Supply and Marketing Corporation on a cooperative basis have sold 358 bicycles, 559 radio sets, 190 sewing machines, and 310 wrist watches to the commune members over the last seven years.

14. *Banking:* The commune members keep their savings with the Credit Cooperative Society. The advances made by the society for home improvement and construction at an annual rate of interest of 4.7 per cent have resulted in 70 per cent of the families having improved dwellings. In all 15,000 new rooms have been constructed with a total floor space of 500,000 sq. meters.

15. *Industry:*

16. *Animal Husbandry:*

17. *Reasons for Success:* The main reasons for the increase in productivity (output of food grain has gone up from 1,139 kg. per hectare in 1957 to 1,359 kg. in 1964 and output of vegetables per hectare has increased from 16,000 kg. in 1957 to 23,000 kg. in 1964) are the successful completion of a network of water conservancy projects and increased scientific use of chemical fertilizer. In 1964, 150 tons of chemical fertilizer were used in the commune.

VII
HSIN LUNG SAN

1. *Date of Formation:* The commune was formed in September, 1958.
   No substantial changes occurred in the period 1959-1961; the commune
   lost only one production brigade to a new commune formed in the east.

2. *Location:* It is situated to the east of Changchun and gets its name from
   the nearby mountain peak. It measures 30 km. from south to north and
   20 km. from east to west. Two railway lines and four paved highways
   connect it with Changchun.

3. *Population:* The commune's 10,130 families have a total population of
   53,270 living in 211 villages. There are 12,790 able-bodied workers
   of whom 7,101 are women.

4. *Land:* Of the 450 sq. km. of communal land, 13,528 hectares are cultivated.

5. *Crops:* The commune has 10,300 hectares under food grain crops and
   2,109 hectares under vegetables. Since 1958, animal husbandry, forestry,
   and fish culture have been successfully adopted as side occupations. In
   1958 there was no systematic cultivation of vegetables; now seven out of
   the commune's twenty brigades specialize in vegetable production.

6. *Sources of Income:* In an average year the commune sells 6,000 tons of
   food grain to the state. This is after meeting the full requirements of its
   members. More than 25 million kg. of vegetables are also supplied. Live
   animals, fish, and table birds provide the commune with additional sources
   of income.

7. *Capital Construction:* Several water conservancy and land improvement
   projects have been completed by the commune since its formation. In
   this period, 96 wells have been dug and six km. of drainage canals have
   been excavated. This has involved earth work equivalent to two million
   cubic meters. With the bringing into operation of 13 pumping stations
   and the installation of 96 electric pumps, the commune has been able to
   bring 550 hectares of land under year round irrigation. Thirteen production

brigades have installed electric cables bringing power to 85 per cent of all the houses in the commune. All the production brigades have been provided with power-operated grain milling machines. The commune has also purchased 11 tractors which now plow 11.2 per cent of the total cultivated land.

8. *Bureaucracy:* Mr. Cheng is the director of the commune. He is 42 years old and has worked in this capacity for five years. He has had no formal education. The county has posted 25 cadres to work in the commune. These cadres receive a total of ¥23,000 per year from the state as wages.

9. *Training in Agriculture:* There are three agricultural middle schools in the commune out of which two are run by production brigades and one by the Education Department of the Commune Secretariat.

10. *Health Facilities:* The commune hospital (30 beds, 6 doctors, 8 nurses) is run by the state. Fifteen production brigades have their own clinics.

11. *Educational Facilities:* The commune's 2 secondary schools and 27 primary schools have a total enrollment of 11,000. There are 200 students in the three agricultural middle schools.

12. *Recreational Facilities:* All production teams have reading rooms.

13. *Marketing:*

14. *Banking:* The commune members deposit their savings in the Credit Cooperative Society. By 1964 the total savings so deposited amounted to ¥10.0 million. No loans have been received by the commune from the society for its land improvement and water conservancy projects. Instead, the Agricultural Bank has been giving every year an amount of ¥400,000 for the execution of these projects.

15. *Industry:* There is no significant industrial activity in the commune. The three repair workshops run by the Commune Management Committee yield an income of ¥6,000 per year.

16. *Animal Husbandry:* There has been a marked increase in the animal population of the commune in the last seven years. In 1958 there were only 2,300 pigs in the commune. Their number has gone up to 11,100.

Apart from these, 20,000 pigs are owned by the families. These families also own nearly 60,000 birds; the number owned by the commune is 450,000. The number of other animals (horses, donkeys, cattle) has increased from 3,350 in 1958 to 4,250 in 1964.

17. *Reasons for Success:* Mr. Cheng cited several indexes to show the ground covered by the commune in the first six years of its existence. The total gross income had gone up from ¥3.8 million in 1958 to ¥6.6 million in 1964. Per capita income in 1958 was ¥57.0; by 1964 it had increased to ¥73.0. Income received per family had gone up from ¥290 in 1958 to ¥386 in 1964; while, in the same period, wages paid out to an able-bodied worker had gone up from ¥240 to ¥309. All this had been achieved by expanding the area of land under cultivation, by providing more water for irrigation, and by increasing the per hectare productivity of cultivated land. In 1958 only 13,000 hectares were cultivated; by 1964 this had increased by 4.6 per cent to 13,528 hectares. No land was irrigated in 1958; 550 hectares of land were assured of regular supply of irrigation water. The yield of food grain had increased from 1,400 kg. per hectare in 1958 to 1,550 kg. in 1964. Similarly, a hectare of land was producing 14,500 kg. of vegetables in 1964 as compared to only 9,000 kg. in 1958. The more spectacular rise in the productivity of vegetables was attributed to a greater use of chemical fertilizer every year. Land under vegetables gets 100 kg. per hectare, leaving hardly anything for grain production. Production had also risen because of a more intensive use of land. In 1958 there were only 8,700 able bodied workers to cutivate 13,000 hectares or 1.5 hectare per worker. In 1964, the land-man ratio had declined to 1.1. Mr. Cheng also attributed the sharp rise in production and levels of incomes to such economic incentives as the better marketability of commodities and higher prices received for them. The price of sorghum has gone up from 10.6 cents per kilo to 13.8 cents per kilo in the six years between 1958 and 1964. Soyabean prices have risen from 19.8 cents per kg. to 23.8 per kg. There has been no change in the price of vegetables.

VIII
PENG PU

1. *Date of Formation:* The commune was formed in September, 1958, with
    the merger of 11 Advanced Agricultural Producers' Cooperatives.

2. *Location:* The commune is situated 13 km. from Shanghai.

3. *Population:* The commune's 3,721 families have a total population of
    17,602. There are 8,552 able bodied workers of whom 5,121 are
    women. The very high proportion of women in the labor force is explained
    by the fact that the commune has released 1,700 workers (mostly men)
    to work in Shanghai's industrial enterprises. Factories channel their demand
    for extra hands to the communes through the Suburban Area Council.
    The commune releases only those who volunteer to go to the city to be
    hired in factories. In 1965, 2,100 workers had volunteered to go to the
    city but only 1,700 were sent because that number adequately met the
    quota alloted to this particular commune by the Suburban Council. About
    half the workers released by the commune in 1965 have continued to live
    in the commune villages; the rest have temporarily migrated to the factory
    premises. The commune reserves the option of calling the released workers
    back at a few months' notice if their presence is required for implementing
    development schemes. Not all the workers released by the commune over
    the years have returned, some 20 per cent have permanently moved to
    the city.

4. *Land:* Out of 1,050 hectares owned by the communes, 958 are cultivated
    all the year round.

5. *Crops:* The commune produces mostly vegetables. Some rice is also grown.
    However, over the years the commune has been able to diversify its
    economy. Commodities sold in the market now include flowers, medicinal
    herbs, mushrooms, dairy products, and pigs. The commune's rice crop
    is just sufficient to meet its own requirements; nothing is left for sale in
    the market. In bad years, rice for home consumption has had to be obtained

'from outside. 1963 was a particularly bad year when a typhoon hit this area. In that year the Suburban Council provided rice at subsidized rates.

6. *Sources of Income:* In 1964, out of a total income of ¥3,861,730 agriculture contributed ¥3,379,296. The rest came from the commune's dairy, pig, seed multiplication, poultry, and mushroom farms. The tractor and implement repairs station contributed ¥7,531 to the gross income.

7. *Capital Construction:* Since its formation, the commune has spent ¥1.0 million on various development projects, including the purchase of farm machinery. In the period 1958-1964, four pumping stations have been built and 122 portable low lift water pumps have been bought by the commune. Pumping stations are maintained by the production brigades and water pumps by the production teams. Brigades and teams pay rent to the Commune Management Committee for the use of this equipment. In the same period the commune has purchased eight tractors while the production teams have acquired 23 hand tillers. Scientific deployment of pumps has brought 90 per cent of the cultivated area under irrigation. The multiple cropping index has also risen from 2.8 in 1957 to 4.0 in 1964. The total expenditure on development projects in 1964 was ¥100,000. This amount was spent on the construction of a bridge, installation of a pumping station, and purchase of a tractor. Only ¥23,000 have been received as loan from the state. This amount has been used for setting up a pig-breeding station (¥8,000), construction of a bridge (¥10,000) and establishing a tractor repair unit (¥5,000).

8. *Bureaucracy:* Mr. Liu is the director and Mr. Chang the deputy director of the commune. The former receives a salary of ¥65.0 per month and the latter ¥45.00 per month. The Commune Management Committee has 17 members of whom six are government cadres. The Commune Secretariat has six departments: Finance and Planning; Health, Education, and Recreation; People's Militia; Civil Affairs; Women's Federation; and Youth League. Each department is headed by a cadre. The commune

has seven other cadres who are not members of the Management Committee. Two work as secretaries in the office of the commune director, two work as accountants in the commune Department of Finance and Planning, one works as an agricultural expert in the agro-technical station, one works as a water conservancy advisor in the Planning Department and one is in charge of the commune Tractor and Implement Repair Workshop.

9. *Training in Agriculture:* The Shanghai Agricultural Academy has set up six demonstration plots in the commune. Supervisory work in these plots is done by the students of the academy. The Suburban Council has set up an agro-technical station which employs seven technicians.

10. *Health Facilities:*

11. *Educational Facilities:*

12. *Recreational Facilities:*

13. *Marketing:*

14. *Banking:*

15. *Industry:*

16. *Animal Husbandry:* The number of pigs multiplied after the pig-breeding station was put into operation. The commune's pig farm has 32,000 animals. There are 10,000 pigs in private ownership. In 1958 the area now under the control of the commune had only 12,000 animals.

17. *Reasons for Success:* In 1952 one *mou* of land yielded only 850 kg. of vegetables. Productivity of land has steadily risen since then. In 1957 it was 3,100 kg. per *mou;* in 1962, 5,818 kg. per *mou;* in 1963 (the year of the typhoon) it went down to 5,453 kg. but rose to a record level of 6,050 kg. in 1964. One main factor responsible for this seven-fold increase in productivity is better water management that has become possible after the installation of pumping stations. Mobile low lift water pumps not only help drain land of excessive water, they also provide water for the area which used to remain completely dry during the dry season. One clear manifestation of the success of the water management program

is the fact that the typhoon of 1963 did not cause any serious disruption in the supply of vegetables to the market. In 1957 (another typhoon year) the vegetable supply was disrupted for more than three months.

IX
HSU HANG

1. *Date of Formation:* The commune was formed in September, 1958, with the amalgamation of thirteen Advanced Agricultural Producers' Cooperatives.
2. *Location:* 50 km. from Shanghai on an unpaved road.
3. *Population:* The commune's 4,649 families have a total population of 17,752. There are 9,149 able-bodied workers of whom 4,589 are men.
4. *Land:* Out of the commune's 1,827 hectares, 1,664 hectares are cultivated.
5. *Crops:* Cotton is the main crop. Rice and wheat are also extensively cultivated. The state had set a procurement target of 650,000 kg. of foodgrains in 1964. Instead the commune was able to supply 1.64 million kg. These three crops account for 85 per cent of the gross income of the commune, the remaining 15 per cent comes from several industrial enterprises. (See below.)
6. *Sources of Income:* See Crops.
7. *Capital Construction:* Various production units have contributed in all ¥2.5 million into the reserve fund. ¥1.7 million have been spent in various development projects. Out of this ¥1.5 million were withdrawn from the reserve fund and ¥200,000 were received from the Agricultural Bank as a long term loan. (Repayments of the loan began in 1963 and in the two years ending 1964, the commune has paid back ¥110,000 to the Agricultural Bank.) An expenditure of ¥214,197 was incurred in 1962, ¥523,660 were spent in 1963 and an outlay of ¥387,000 was made in 1964. The commune has built twenty-seven pumping stations and helped production teams procure nineteen mobile pumps. The commune has also purchased five 25 hp tractors for which it has paid ¥50,000 in all. It has also bought three trucks for ¥52,000. (A 10 hp mobile pump costs ¥3,000.) State assistance was used for building food grain storage godowns at five different places. All the godowns are located on canal banks and grain is loaded into boats straight from the godowns.

8. *Bureaucracy:* Mr. Wang, the director of the commune, was elected to this post immediately after the formation of the commune. He heads a management committee that has a total membership of twenty-five, including eleven government cadres. The Commune Secretariat has eight departments, each supervised by a cadre who is also a member of the Management Committee. The departments are Agricultural Development; Finance, Planning, and Accounting; Education, Health and Recreation; Factory Management; Civil Affairs; Youth Leagues; Women's Federation; and Civil Militia. The commune's Supervisory Committee also has four cadres.

9. *Training in Agriculture:* The commune's one agro-technical station has trained forty-two technicians since its formation in 1962. It is run by a graduate in agriculture who is paid by the county council.

10. *Health Facilities:* The commune has a 22-bed hospital located in a house owned at the time of liberation by a landlord to whom belonged more than 1,000 hectares of cultivated land. The six-bedroom mansion was converted into a hospital by the commune with the help of a health technician sent by the county council. All but two of the commune's production brigades have their own health clinics. The main villages of the production brigades without health clinics are very near the commune hospital. An out-patient section has been provided in the main hospital to meet the requirements of the people belonging to those production brigades. The commune's three surgeons have performed over 600 major and minor operations since 1962.

11. *Educational Facilities:* The commune has one secondary school, two middle schools and 23 primary schools. The total enrollment in all these institutions is 2827 of whom 1142 are girls.

12. *Recreational Facilities:*

13. *Marketing:* All the 127 production teams have their own retail shops. The biggest retail shop is located at Hsu Hang village. This shop has a warehouse which is used by all the other retail shops. Trucks from Shanghai

bring consumer goods to the Hsu Hang shop; these goods are redistributed to other shops from there.

14. *Banking:* The peasants deposit their savings in the six branches of the Credit Cooperative Society.

15. *Industry:* The commune has a workshop for the manufacture and repair of farm implements, a straw-mat weaving factory and a towel-making factory. These industrial enterprises employ 458 workers. The average income of an industrial worker is ¥50 compared to ¥21 received on the average by agricultural workers.

16. *Animal Husbandry:*

17. *Reasons for Success:* The productivity of land has steadily increased since 1949, the year this area was fully liberated by the Communists. However, the increase in productivity has been more spectacular since 1958, the year of communization of agriculture. In 1949 a hectare of land produced 3,255 kg. of rice, or 877 kg. of wheat, or 150 kg. of cotton. By 1957 productivity of land had increased by about 40 per cent and in that year a hectare of land produced 3,870 kg. of rice, or 1,177 kg. of wheat or 285 kg. of raw cotton. In 1963, which was a bad year since much of the commune land was flooded, a hectare of land produced 6,105 kg. of rice, or 1,957 kg. of wheat or 607 kg. of cotton. In 1964 output of land had considerably increased: 7,275 kg. of rice or 2,910 kg. of wheat or 855 kg. of cotton were obtained from one hectare of cultivated land. The director of the commune assigned the following seven reasons for this steady increase in the productivity of the soil: a) leadership of the party and the state had presented the people of the commune with common goals which could be achieved with concentrated effort, b) the state had provided financial and technical assistance to the commune to solve some of its major problems, c) better planning of the utilization of the commune's output had made it possible for the production units to implement several development schemes from their own resources, d) installation of pumping stations and purchase of mobile water

pumps had made it possible for the production units to tackle the problem of water logging, e) state help had also made it possible for the peasants to adopt new scientific methods of cultivation, f) the state had made available new inputs like chemical fertilizer and insecticides. No chemical fertilizer was being used in 1950; in 1964 all the production units in the commune used 460 tons of ammonium sulphate and ammonium water, g) the plans drawn up by the state had helped the commune dispose of its surplus agricultural produce at good prices.

X
WEST LAKE

1. *Date of Formation:* The commune was formed in September, 1958, with
   the amalgamation of twenty tea-producing cooperatives. In 1961 the
   original commune was split in two; West Lake Commune inherited fourteen
   of the twenty-six production brigades. The remaining twelve production
   brigades were merged with three others to form the biggest and most
   prosperous of the tea-producing communes in Hangchow.
2. *Location:* 15 km. from Hangchow in hilly country.
3. *Population:* The commune's 1,800 families have a total population of
   8,000 living in eleven villages. There are 4,800 able-bodied workers.
4. *Land:* The commune has 333 hectares of cultivated land. No estimate of
   the total land available to the commune has so far been made.
5. *Crops:* The commune has 200 hectares of land under tea. Out of this 188
   hectares have matured tea plants while 12 hectares have only very recently
   been planted with tea shrubs. Rice is grown in 70 hectares. A three-hectare
   farm produces jasmine flowers for use in the commune's jasmine tea-making
   factory.
6. *Sources of Income:* Tea is sold to the state in blended form. For this
   purpose the commune has set up fourteen tea-processing factories. Of
   the total income of ¥1,755,650, 80 per cent comes from the sale of
   blended tea to the state. The director has no idea of the value added in
   the tea-processing plants.
7. *Capital Construction:* A total investment of ¥1.17 million has been
   made in development projects in the period 1958-1964. Out of this only
   ¥570,000 have come from the commune's own savings; ¥60,000 have
   been given by the Agricultural Bank. In 1964 the commune had only
   ¥13,000 in the reserve fund. The bulk of the expenditure has been on
   the provision of machinery for the tea-processing factories. Forty thousand
   yuan have also been spent on the installation of electric cables to bring

power to the factories. All the houses in the commune have also been provided with electric power.

8. *Bureaucracy:* The Commune Management Committee has eleven members of whom four are government cadres. These include the director (Mr. Chung); the deputy director, who is also in charge of the Department of Finance, Planning and Accounting; the head of the Department of Factory Management; and the head of the Department of People's Militia.

9. *Training in Agriculture:* The local county council has set up a special center to give training in tea growing, leaf plucking, and tea blending. Fourteen special teams of women, each under the charge of a production brigade, are responsible for plucking leaves. All the team leaders and 25 per cent of all the members have received training at the center. This training program has not only increased the number of leaves plucked per hour per person but also eliminated any chance of damage to the tea shrubs. The tea-blending instructor in the center is from the commune. He received his training in Hangchow. He has been able to introduce the production of various kinds of flower-scented teas in the commune.

10. *Health Facilities:* The commune has no in-patient hospital. Patients requiring hospitalization are sent to Hangchow. Seven health clinics serve all fourteen production brigades. An Institute of Traditional Chinese Medicine is located very near the commune. Fifty-two commune members have been treated in the institute over the last four years. (The institute is housed in a modern four-story building. It has provision for 150 indoor patients. We were taken around the institute by its director, a sixty-year-old man who has practiced traditional medicine for the last thirty years.)

11. *Educational Facilities:* The commune has 2,400 students going to its thirteen schools. There are three middle and ten primary schools. The commune is proposing to convert one of the middle schools into a secondary school.

12. *Recreational Facilities:*

13. *Marketing:*

14. *Banking:*

15. *Industry:* (Also see under "Sources of Income.") Of the commune's fourteen tea-blending factories, eight are mechanized. Six use hand-operated machines and produce flower-scented tea leaves. According to the cadre in charge of the commune Department of Factory Management, "flower tea" cannot be produced by machines alone. It is a delicate operation requiring not only expertise in handling tea leaves and flowers but also a very fine sense of smell.

16. *Animal Husbandry:* See below.

17. *Reasons for Success:* Over the years, yields per hectare of tea as well as rice have steadily increased. In 1947 a hectare of land produced only 347 kg. of dry tea leaves. In 1957, a year before the formation of the commune, the yield per hectare had gone up to 1,200 kg., an increase of over 260 per cent. Output per hectare has gone on increasing after communization; in 1964 it had gone up to 1,950 kg. This increase in output has been accomplished in mainly three ways: better terracing of tea fields to ensure a more effective and scientific use of water, adoption of improved tea cultivation and leaf plucking methods (see "Training in Agriculture," above), and an intensive use of chemical fertilizer. The use of fertilizer per hectare of tea-growing land has gone up ten times in the four-year period between 1960 and 1964; in 1962 only 100 kg. of ammonium sulphate were being applied per hectare but in 1964 this had increased to 1,000 kg. There has also been an increase in the yield of rice-growing land. In 1947 it was only 1,125 kg. per hectare, in 1957 it increased to 3,675 kg. and in 1964 it reached the record level of 7,950 kg. However, little chemical fertilizer has been used for rice cultivation. For rice, sheep dung manure is being produced. The commune has sixteen flocks of sheep with a total population of 7,500. One sheep produces one ton of manure per year.

XI
TUNG CHUN

1. *Date of Formation:* The commune was formed in September, 1958.

2. *Location:* About 84 km. from Hangchow on the Hachan River. (A visit to this commune had not been planned for us. It was arranged by the officials of the Chekiang Department of Agriculture after it had been suggested to them that the delegation would like to see a commune which the Chinese officials regarded as a real success story. Tung Chun Commune has come a long way but still remains relatively poor; its per capita income was lower than all the other communes seen by us.)

3. *Population:* The commune's 2,014 families have a total population of 9,316 of whom 5,112 are able-bodied workers.

4. *Land:* Out of the commune's total area of 13,000 hectares, only 588 hectares are cultivated. The rest lies barren and is subject to occasional floods.

5. *Crops:* Previously only dry land crops (sorghum and millet) were grown. Now rice is the main crop. Green manure crops are also grown to improve soil fertility.

6. *Sources of income:* In 1964 the commune sold one million kg. of food grains to the state. (Until 1961 this was a food deficit area; the state used to supply 150,000 kg. of food grains every year at heavily subsidized rates.) 823,000 kg. of fruits are also produced every year. The commune owns two fruit canning factories. A sheep farm has 10,000 animals that produce 8,000 tons of manure for use in the commune. Unprocessed wool is also sold in the market. Ten per cent of the gross income comes from the sale of processed fruit and wool to the State Trading Corporation.

7. *Capital Construction:* In the seven years since its formation, the commune has been able to accumulate only ¥350,000 in the reserve fund. All of this amount has been spent on various development projects; in addition the commune has received ¥250,000 from the Agricultural Bank. Projects

completed so far include two earth and three stone embankments with a total length of 5.5 km.; eleven water reservoirs with a total storage capacity of 1.1 million cubic meters, 49 irrigation channels with a total length of 70 km.; and eight open surface wells in the land which cannot be reached by river water. Eight pumpting stations feed the reservoirs and 49 low lift pumps facilitate the movement of water from the reservoirs, through channels and into the fields. All the pumps are driven with electricty; the commune has sold 11 diesel pumps to the state which used to bring water from the river before electric power reached the commune area. The assistance received from the Agricultural Bank has been used mostly for conveying electricity to the pumping stations. For this purpose, nine transformers have been installed. Ninety per cent of the cultivated land can now depend upon an assured supply of irrigation water all the year round.

8. *Bureaucracy:* The Commune Management Committee has fifteen members of whom seven, including the commune director, are cadres. The director, Mr. Chu, has held this office for the last five years; before coming to the commune he was employed by the Hangchow Town Council. Mr. Chu was elected to his third term in January, 1964, by the Commune Congress, by a vote of 99-11. Mr. Liu, the deputy-director, held the commune directorship before Mr. Chu joined the commune. In 1960 the election for directorship was contested by Mr. Chu and Mr. Liu. The former received 83 votes and the latter 35. Mr. Chu is 42; Mr. Liu is 57. Mr. Liu is a government cadre but has never served outside the commune. Before the formation of the commune he was in charge of an Advanced Agricultural Producers' Cooperative. The commune took off economically after the change in directorship. One reason for the greater effectiveness of Mr. Chu could be that he was able to bring in greater state assistance for the development of this area. His contacts with the Hangchow bureaucracy must have helped him.

9. *Training in Agriculture:* The commune has developed an elaborate system of training its members in agriculture. There are organized agricultural research groups at all the three levels; i.e., the commune, production brigade and production team. The commune group is made up of nine persons, four of whom are old and experienced farmers, four are young farmers who have graduated from the commune's Agricultural Middle School, and one is a technician provided by the local county council. This group undertakes "variety and fertilizer" tests and has a one-and-a-half hectare plot allotted to it for this purpose. The brigade level research groups are similarly constituted but they do not have any technician attached to them. These groups also have their special purpose plots. There are no permanently organized research groups at the production team level. However, students from the Hangchow Agricultural College visit the production teams and work on the production team experimental plots for three months. We met with one such production team research group. It had three members, one a veterinarian, another a plant protection specialist and the third a mechanic. New chemical fertilizers, seeds, etc., are tested by the commune and production brigade groups simultaneously. The results of these tests are passed on to the students working in the production teams for verification. Since the students work closely with the farmers, the latter automatically learn to use successful new inputs.

10. *Health Facilities:* The commune has one ten-bed hospital and eight health clinics.

11. *Educational Facilities:* The commune has four secondary schools, one Agriculture Middle School and thirteen primary schools. Total enrollment in these institutions is 1,840. There are thirty-six students (twenty-two boys and fourteen girls) belonging to the commune who are enrolled in the Hangchow University.

12. *Recreational Facilities:*

13. *Marketing:* The State Supply and Marketing Corporation has set up twenty-one retail shops, one for each production team. In the last seven years the

members of the commune have bought 121 bicycles, 153 radio sets, 102 alarm clocks, 52 sewing machines, and 82 wrist watches.

14. *Banking:* All the 2,014 commune families have opened accounts with the Credit Cooperative Society. With the help of the loans advanced by the society, the commune members have been able to construct 496 new rooms at a total cost of ¥240,000.

15. *Industry:* See "Sources of Income."

16. *Animal Husbandry:* See "Sources of Income."

17. *Reasons for Success:* The yield of rice has increased from 1,500 kg. per hectare obtained in 1949 to 7,530 kg. per hectare produced in 1964. The director cited three main reasons for this remarkable progress: a) the scientific development of the commune's water resources has made it possible to grow improved varieties of rice, b) it has been possible to introduce new inputs and farming techniques fairly quickly with the help of an elaborate research outfit, c) improved management of private plots by the farmers has added to the overall productivity of the commune.

XII
PEOPLE'S SUBURBAN

1. *Date of Formation:* The commune was formed in July, 1961, just before the start of the fishing season, with the amalgamation of five fishermen's production brigades. In 1958, at the time of communization in China, production brigades rather than communes had been formed in this area. This policy was reversed in 1961.

2. *Location:* The commune is located on the banks of Lake Tai Ho near Wusih in Kiangsu Province. The lake has a surface area of 2,200 sq. km. and has five communes situated on its banks.

3. *Population:* The commune's 553 families have a total population of 2,753 of whom 1,365 are able-bodied workers.

4. *Land:* The commune owns no cultivable land of its own. Fishermen have small plots attached to their houses in which they grow vegetables and keep pigs and fowls. The commune has a fishing region demarcated within the lake. The boats owned by the commune are not allowed to go beyond this region. The demarcation of the region was done by the Lake Management Committee. (See "Bureaucracy".)

5. *Crops:*

6. *Sources of Income:* Fishing is the only communal source of income. In 1964 the total catch was 13.75 million kg.

7. *Capital Construction:* Various production units have deposited a total of ¥250,000 in the commune reserve fund since its formation in 1961. In the same period the commune has invested ¥400,000 in various development projects. These include a fishing wharf (¥120,000), purchase of thirty-eight new boats (¥200,000), and purchase of nylon fishing nets (¥30,000). The state has advanced ¥200,000 to the commune through the Aquatic Products Corporation. A boat of the type obtained by the commune costs ¥5,250. In one fishing season (August-April), one boat is able to haul, on an average, ¥7,700 worth of fish.

8. *Bureaucracy:* The Commune Management Committee has fifteen members of whom six, including Mr. Hsu, the director of the commune, are government cadres. The non-official group within the Management Committee is made up of four old and experienced fishermen, two young fishermen who have received special training in fishing and net weaving, and two women. The commune has no cadres working outside the Management Committee. The Production Brigade Management Committees have one leader, two deputy leaders and six ordinary members. The director and deputy director of the commune are also the members of the Lake Management Committee. This committee has a membership of twenty-two, drawn from all the five communes located on the lake's banks and from the Fisheries Departments of Kiangsu, Chekiang, and Suchow Provinces. The main function of the committee is to allocate regions within the lake to the various communes.

9. *Training in Agriculture:* See "Educational Facilities."

10. *Health Facilities:* The commune has a mobile (boat) clinic.

11. *Educational Facilities:* The commune has only one primary school with a total enrollment of 180 boys and girls. The commune has also set up a work-study school. It is located on a big boat which can accommodate thirty children. The children are taught to weave and cast fishing nets, to manage boats, etc., and, at the same time, are given instruction in reading, writing, and arithmetic. This type of education has proved tremendously successful and the commune is actively considering purchasing another boat to start a similar institution.

12. *Recreational Facilities:*

13. *Marketing:* The commune has two mobile (boat) shops. These move from one lakeside village to another selling their wares. The State Supply and Marketing Corporation is now considering setting up a shop in the main village of the commune. This shop would also supply goods to the mobile shops.

14. *Banking:* The Credit Cooperative Society has one office located in the same building as the office of the commune director. Its total deposits amount to ¥50,000.

15. *Industry:* The commune has made an application to the Aquatic Products Corporation for funds to finance a cold storage and a fish-drying plant. The application was made in July 1964. The corporation is likely to agree to the setting up of a fish-drying plant. ("Likely" because nothing has been heard through the official channel. However, Mr. Hsu was told recently by an official that the corporation was taking steps to advance a loan of ¥25,000 to the commune for this purpose.) The commune's future plans include adding a packing unit to serve the cold storage and drying plants. The packing unit would be financed out of the savings in the reserve fund. However, all this depends upon whether or not the commune receives assistance for the two plants from the corporation, in the first place. The commune expects an increase of 20 per cent in its gross income after the entire industrial development program has been implemented. (In Wusih we made inquiries about the fate of this industrial program. The official in charge of planning in the Aquatic Products Corporation told us that the entire program, including the setting up of a semi-mechanized packing plant, had been approved. The corporation was coordinating the programs drawn up by all the lakeside communes. The coordinated program would include the setting up of fish-drying plants in three of the five communes, cold storages in all the five communes, and packing units in two communes. All these units would provide employment to 750 fishermen. The corporation was giving high priority to the program because of a 2.5 per cent per annum rate of increase in the population of these communes since 1961. The fishing potential of Lake Tai Ho would not allow the full utilization of additonal labor which was becoming available in the communes. Industrialization of the communes would, therefore, diversify their economies and afford new avenues of employment to the commune members.)

16. *Animal Husbandry:*

17. *Reasons for Success:* The director of the commune was satisfied with
the progress made since 1961. However, he did not provide any concrete
evidence of this progress. For instance, he did not have the figures for the
total catch in 1961 or 1962 or the amount of total haul made by a single
boat in those years. Before Liberation, the fishermen, according to
Mr. Hsu, used to go about in rags and used twigs in place of chopsticks.
In 1964 all the fishermen were properly attired and presumably had also
acquired chopsticks.

XIII
STONEWELL

1. *Date of Formation:* The commune was formed in October, 1958, and was reorganized in 1960.

2. *Location:* 20 km. from Canton in the province of Kwangtung.

3. *Population:* The commune's 11,900 families have a total population of 43,000 of whom 22,000 are able-bodied workers.

4. *Land:* Out of a total area of 89 sq. km., only 3,000 hectares are cultivated. Most of the commune's area is low lying and suffers from occasional floods.

5. *Crops:* Rice, sugar cane, and wheat are the main crops. Vegetables are also grown.

6. *Sources of Income:* Only 62 per cent of the commune's gross income comes from agriculture, the remaining 38 per cent comes from such diverse sources as industries, fisheries, animal husbandry, and transport.

7. *Capital Construction:* A total of ¥13.5 million has been spent in various development projects since the formation of the commune. Out of this ¥8.5 million were spent by the Commune Management Committee and ¥5.0 million by production brigades and production teams. The commune and other production units have spent only ¥3.7 million from their own sources; the rest has been received from the state as grant-in-aid and low interest, long-term loans. From the help received from the state, ¥540,000 have been spent by the Commune Management Committee and ¥8.26 million by the production brigades and teams. In the period 1958-1964, the commune acquired and set up for its various production units, forty-one pumping stations and 230 mobile electric pumps. The pumps can quickly free the fields of inundation and also, during periods of draught, can bring water into the fields. At the same time the commune has installed a mechanized brick kiln, a lime factory, four agricultural implements and tractor repair shops, a central grain-processing mill, five pig farms, eighteen poultry farms, six fruit tree nurseries, and six fish fry farms. These activities

have increased the commune's income from ¥700,000 in 1958 to ¥2.1 million in 1964. (This does not include the incomes of production brigades and teams.)

8. *Bureaucracy:* The Commune Management Committee has seventeen members of whom nine, including the director and two deputy directors, are cadres. The Commune Secretariat has eleven departments responsible for Finance and Accounting; Development Planning; Civil Affairs; Civil Militia; Health, Education and Recreation; Women's Federation; Youth Leagues; Agricultural Training; Fisheries, Animal Husbandry and Horti- culture; Industries; and Water Management. All departments have cadres in charge; some cadres are responsible for more than one department. Six production brigades have also been assigned cadres; there are in all nine cadres working in these production brigades. In all these production brigades, management committees are headed by the cadres. There are in all twenty-three cadres working in the various communal organizations.

9. *Training in Agriculture:* An elaborate but totally decentralized system for imparting training in agriculture to the farmers has been devised. Under this all the 150 production teams have experimental plots measuring from one half of a hectare to one-and-a-half hectares. These plots carry out experiments either on their own initiative or on receiving direction from the commune's Department of Agricultural Training. We were provided with one rather unusual piece of evidence of the impact of these experimental plots on the use of inputs in agriculture. In 1962, on an average, 22 kg. of insecticides were being used on one hectare of cultivated land. In 1964, only 15 kg. were used. This decrease has been made possible by a technique of treating seeds before sowing. The technique was developed in the experimental plots. Treatment of seeds reduces the chances of plant disease infestation.

10. *Health Facilities:* The commune has a big 45-bed hospital located in a new building completed only a year ago. At the time of our visit to the hospital, 39 beds were occupied. The hospital has one house surgeon

and two house physicians. All production brigades and six production teams have their own clinics. The commune has also set up a large poor people's home. The home is located in a paper-making factory which was closed in 1961. It houses forty old people who are provided with food, clothing, medical care, and recreational facilities. This is the only institute of its type that we saw in China.

11. *Educational Facilities:*

12. *Recreational Facilities:* All the production brigades and teams have reading rooms. These are supplied with the liteature that the commune management receives free from the county government. The commune is still operating a community dining room. Thirteen such rooms were set up after the formation of the commune; all but one were closed in 1960. The dining room is located near the commune's factory area. It has facilities for catering to seventy-five people at the same time. The people eating in the dining room pay for their meals. However, the commune gives a subsidy of ¥1,000 out of the welfare fund to the dining room.

13. *Marketing:* The State Supply and Marketing Corporation has set up 161 retail shops in the commune. These stores have sold 1,396 bicycles, 3,210 radio sets, 2,520 alarm clocks, 2,010 wrist watches, 52,000 fountain pens and 120,000 aluminum utensils to the members of the commune.

14. *Banking:* The commune members deposit their savings with the Credit Cooperative Society. By 1964, the commune members had deposited ¥898,000 in the seven branches of the society. Three thousand new homes had been built with the help of the advances received from the society.

15. *Industry:* Many new industries were set up in 1958. These included paper-making, cement-manufacturing, and pottery-making enterprises. Almost all of them have now ceased to function. We were shown a mechanized brick kiln which was set up by the commune in 1961 at a cost of ¥6,000. The labor liberated as a result of the winding up of the industrial units

has been sent to work in the factories of Canton. All the surplus labor in the commune is sent to the city for industrial or commercial employment. Requisitions for labor are regularly received from the city and are handled by the management of the production brigades.

INDEX

HARVARD EAST ASIAN MONOGRAPHS

18. Frank H. H. King (ed.) and Prescott Clarke, *A Research Guide to China-Coast Newspapers, 1822-1911*

19. Ellis Joffe, *Party and Army: Professionalism and Political Control in the Chinese Officer Corps, 1949-1964*

20. Toshio G. Tsukahira, *Feudal Control in Tokugawa Japan: The Sankin Kōtai System*

21. Kwang-Ching Liu, ed., *American Missionaries in China: Papers from Harvard Seminars*

22. George Moseley, *A Sino-Soviet Cultural Frontier: The Ili Kazakh Autonomous Chou*

23. Carl F. Nathan, *Plague Prevention and Politics in Manchuria, 1910-1931*

24. Adrian Arthur Bennett, *John Fryer: The Introduction of Western Science and Technology into Nineteenth-Century China*

25. Donald J. Friedman, *The Road from Isolation: The Campaign of the American Committee for Non-Participation in Japanese Aggression, 1938-1941*

26. Edward Le Fevour, *Western Enterprise in Late Ch'ing China: A Selective Survey of Jardine, Matheson and Company's Operations, 1842-1895*

27. Charles Neuhauser, *Third World Politics: China and the Afro-Asian People's Solidarity Organization, 1957-1967*

28. Kungtu C. Sun, assisted by Ralph W. Huenemann, *The Economic Development of Manchuria in the First Half of the Twentieth Century*

29. Shahid Javed Burki. *A Study of Chinese Communes, 1965*